Come and
I Will Sing You

A NEWFOUNDLAND SONGBOOK

Edited by Genevieve Lehr

Songs collected by
Genevieve Lehr and Anita Best

Breakwater, St John's, Newfoundland

© University of Toronto Press 1985
Toronto Buffalo London
Printed in Canada
ISBN 0-8020-2567-6 (cloth)
ISBN 0-8020-6586-4 (paper)

Co-published in the Atlantic Provinces
by Breakwater Books
in Canada's Atlantic Folklore-Folklife Series
ISBN 0919519-79-2 (cloth)
ISBN 0919519-77-6 (paper)

Canadian Cataloguing in Publication Data

Main entry under title:
Come and I will sing you
Includes index.

ISBN 0-8020-2567-6 (bound).
ISBN 0-8020-6586-4 (pbk.)
1. Folk-songs, English – Newfoundland.
I. Lehr, Genevieve, 1956-   II. Best, Anita.
M1678.C672 1985   784.4 '9718   C85-098672-9

Illustrations by Elly Cohen

Musical transcriptions by Pamela Morgan

Music copied by Robin Charles

This book has been published
with the help of a generous gift to the
University of Toronto Press from
the Herbert Laurence Rous Estate, and
block grants from the Canada Council
and the Ontario Arts Council.

Contents

Contributors

Ernest Barter, Ramea, Southwest Coast
Emile Benoit, Port au Port Peninsula
Anita Best, St John's
Elsie Best, St John's
Carrie Brennan, Ship Cove, Placentia Bay
Gerald Campbell, Branch, St Mary's Bay
Jack Carroll, Stephenville
Margaret Carroll, Ramea, Southwest Coast
Mary (Min) Caul, Arnold's Cove, Placentia Bay
John Joe English, Branch, St Mary's Bay
Annie Felix, Port au Port Peninsula
Bill Foley, Tilting, Fogo Island
Philip Foley, Tilting, Fogo Island
Jerry Fudge, McCallum, Southwest Coast
Annie Green, Francois, Southwest Coast
Isaac Harris, St John's
Moses Harris, Lethbridge, Bonavista Bay
John Hayman, Ramea, Southwest Coast
Ray Hepditch, Southeast Bight, Placentia Bay
Maurice Hogan, Flatrock, Conception Bay
Benedict Keough, Plate Cove, Bonavista Bay
Cyril Keough, Plate Cove, Bonavista Bay
Mick Keough, Plate Cove, Bonavista Bay
John (Jack) Lushman, Sr, Ramea, Southwest Coast
Frankie Nash, Branch, St Mary's Bay
Rosy Northcott, Ramea, Southwest Coast
Kitty O'Shaughnessey, Kingman's Cove, Fermeuse
Jim Payne, St John's
Johnny Tobias Pearson, Southeast Bight, Placentia Bay
Lillian Pittman, Placentia, Placentia Bay
Pius Power, Jr, Southeast Bight, Placentia Bay
Pius Power, Sr, Southeast Bight, Placentia Bay
Dorman Ralph, St John's
Guillaume (Willie) Robin, Port au Port Peninsula
Bride Rose, Freshwater, Placentia Bay
Val Ryan, St John's
Mary Ann Skinner, Francois, Southwest Coast
Linda Slade, St John's
Anthony Ward, St John's
Edward Ward, Southeast Bight, Placentia Bay
Kate Wilson, Placentia, Placentia Bay

Preface

My intention in presenting these songs is to provide a handy reference for people who want to learn and sing them. The melodies have not been altered in any way, although the keys of some have been transposed so that they will be easier to read and sing. Where this change occurs, the original key of the singer has been cited below the song. With the texts I have taken a few small liberties. If a singer forgot verses or lines, the song was completed in most cases with words from another singer's version in our collection rather than from versions in printed texts.

The songs I have chosen are taken mainly from tape-recordings that Anita Best and I made from 1975 to 1983; a few were given to us by people who had written them down because tunes did not yet exist for them. I have placed particular emphasis on songs of local composition, although the 120 selected here are a cross-section of all the songs we collected and thus include many that settlers brought with them to Newfoundland from Europe. Some of the local songs may not be as aesthetically pleasing to the uninitiated, but they are cherished by the singers who so graciously and joyfully sang them for us. Like Elizabeth Greenleaf in *Ballads and Sea Songs of Newfoundland*, we recognize 'that the precious "literary quality" which we collectors seek in ballads is a very secondary thing to the folk who compose and sing them ...' The local songs are, so to speak, still in the making; their history is relatively short compared to that of the European ballads presented in this collection, and they are still being modified and shaped in and by the oral tradition that created them.

I have not, as a rule, included songs that can be found in the four major collections of Newfoundland songs, namely, *Folksongs from Newfoundland* by Maud Karpeles; *Songs of the Newfoundland Outports* by Kenneth Peacock; *Songs of the Lower Labrador Coast* by MacEdward Leach; and *Ballads and Sea Songs of Newfoundland* by Elizabeth Bristol Greenleaf and Grace Yarrow Mansfield. Exceptions were made for songs having either texts or airs different from those found in these collections; a page number from Paul Mercer's *Newfoundland Songs and Ballads in Print, 1842–1974; a title and first-line index* has been provided below the accompanying note to these variants for anyone wishing to do a comparative study.

In the course of transcribing the texts from the tapes I encountered a good many words completely unfamiliar to me. In some instances I was enlightened by a dictionary of standard English or by the *Dictionary of Newfoundland English*. For the rest, I wrote them as I thought they should be spelled, often acting on suggestions from Anita Best or faculty members of Memorial University's Linguistics Department. In some cases I have included interpretations of their meanings given by the singers themselves. Some of these words or expressions are included in the Glossary of Unfamiliar Words at the back of the book.

In dealing with the various dialects of the singers, I decided to include the non-standard grammatical features used by the singers (for example, 'we was' instead of 'we were'; 'she runned' or 'run' instead of 'she ran'), but only those non-standard features of pronunciation necessary to the rhyme and rhythm of the songs. If I had used non-standard spelling to indicate every unusual feature of these dialects, the reader would be struggling to unravel the orthographic mystery before ever getting the sense of the story, and this book would lose its value as a songbook. Excellent commentary on dialect features of Newfoundland English may be found in *A Dialect Survey of Carbonear, Newfoundland* by Dr Harold Paddock of Memorial University and in the introduction to the *Dictionary of Newfoundland English.*

Historical notes and other information about the songs were gathered from various sources: the Centre for Newfoundland Studies, Queen Elizabeth II Library, Memorial University of Newfoundland; the A.C. Hunter Library in St John's; the Folklore Department Archives at Memorial University; and, most importantly, from the singers who contributed to this collection. Very often, while browsing absent-mindedly through a book or magazine, I would unexpectedly find a wealth of information; or during conversations with friends and acquaintances, a simple 'Did you ever hear the song about the ...' would inevitably draw forth facts and stories I had long been searching for.

To the joint acknowledgments that follow I would like to add here my thanks to my co-workers: Pamela Morgan, whose own musical creativity and intuitive feel for folk music has given these songs new life; Elly Cohen, who so masterfully captured the visual essence of the songs; and Anita Best, whose love and respect for the folksongs and music of Newfoundland and Labrador inspired me to decide, so many years ago, some day to present these songs in book form.

Genevieve Lehr
St John's 1985

Introduction

When I was growing up in Placentia Bay I often heard songs at weddings, soup suppers, and similar gatherings in people's kitchens and parish halls. They captured my imagination at the time, but held little meaning for me. After all, you never heard them on the radio, except on Saturday mornings when The Big Six, 'Once a number, now an institution,' would present its weekly offering of 'Irish' music: the McNulty Family, Jimmy Shand, Carmel O'Quinn, Omar Blondahl (alias Sagebrush Sam), and occasionally John White. This program often stirred up tremendous controversy among the Saturday morning floor-scrubbing circles. 'The Wild Colonial Boy' was a hot subject: some claimed the radio version had the wrong facts concerning Jack Duggan; some even went so far as to argue that his name wasn't

Jack Duggan at all. Just about everyone was in agreement that the air was all wrong. I listened to these mysterious disputes with only one ear, because I was hoping they'd put on 'Roses Are Blooming' or 'The Mountie's Prayer.' Pretty soon the Carter Family and Hank Snow gave way to Patsy Cline and Jim Reeves. We sang the Hank Williams songs with the most intense devotion, although there was always a vague uneasiness on us – it was the kind of feeling you get when you pretend not to recognize someone you know across the street.

In the 1950s and 1960s we jumped headlong into the sea of rock 'n roll. Our parents hated it, so we loved it all the more. We'd never be caught dead listening to the 'Newfie' music they played on VOCM.

The old songs persisted, though, and we were mildly surprised when we found ourselves enjoying them at dances or caught ourselves humming a few verses as we waited for busses. Then along came the Clancy Brothers, Joan Baez, Peter, Paul and Mary, and the folk revival of the sixties. Suddenly, the old songs we half-knew rose to the surface. They had merely been biding their time. With a prod from Fairport Convention, Steeleye Span, and Planxty we began to examine and delight in our own songs. We talked about them all the time, wrote down versions from our aunts and grandmothers, and passed them along to our friends. We discovered Maud Karpeles, Kenneth Peacock, and Greenleaf and Mansfield. We listened to Laverne Squires singing 'Who Is at My Window Weeping' and we wept; we heard Ronnie Tilley singing 'The Bloody Gardener' and we fell victim.

Then I met Genevieve Lehr, and was delighted to find that she had the same interest and delight in the old songs as myself. In 1976 we decided to try to capture some of these songs on tape before they all began to go underground again. Armed with a Sony Cassette and an eccentric old Telefunken tape-recorder borrowed from the Memorial University Folklore Archive, we went our separate ways to Bonavista Bay and Placentia Bay and the Southwest Coast. During those trips we met John Joe and Mon English, Uncle Mose Harris, Pius Power, and a great many other wonderful people. We didn't collect as much as we might have, but we became involved in the lives of those people, and they became a part of our lives.

Since we were interested in the singer's approach to folksongs we did not exclude any songs from our taping, but recorded anything and everything that was sung for us. Consequently, we ended up with an awful lot of material that had been learned from recordings or radio broadcasts. These tunes were quite popular with both the singer and the audience, the latter often joining in with great enthusiasm. Most singers made no distinction between these and other songs, finding one to be just as good as another. We do not make any aesthetic judgments, but we have retained only the ones that derived from oral tradition, as far as we could find out.

There were songs that we weren't allowed to tape because the singer thought they were 'treason songs.' These were usually ones showing racial or religious prejudices, or ones ridiculing, even slandering, people still alive or with close relatives still living. Although they were sung privately, for whatever reasons the singers would never sing them at a public gathering. We found ourselves of the same opinion and have not included any in this collection.

The repertoires of the singers varied greatly, both in size and content, and were continually changing. Songs were forgotten and discarded or were updated. We noticed that several singers were beginning to use guitar or accordion accompaniments.

Some of the songs in this book were sung in kitchens with numerous young children more or less restrained by some sympathetic relative. Some were recorded on stage heads and in trap stores while the singer was knitting twine or repairing a lobster pot. Some were recorded aboard ship, either at anchor or en route to some small deserted harbour in Placentia Bay. The blowers of oilstoves, clattering supper dishes, and boat engines were a constant bane.

Some of the singers were very interested in the machines we were using and punctuated their songs with comments and questions about this wonderful process. One singer wanted to hear every song played back two or three times after he had sung it. One singer, eighty-five years old, was so distressed by her own singing when she heard it played back that she refused to sing any more songs for us; perhaps she was remembering the magnificent performances of her youth which lived on in the hearts of her appreciative neighbours and friends. A fair number of people who sang for us were quick to point out that they were 'no good to sing' and that we would be wasting our tape. Some of these were not falsely modest, but others gave us the most beautiful songs in the collection. There was the scattered person who thought we were completely wasting our time, that nobody would be interested in such 'old randoms,' but they freely sang, for whatever it was worth. One crafty old man wouldn't sing for the tape-recorder because he thought we would play his songs on the radio and amass a rapid fortune with them. One very sensitive old gentleman thought that recording the songs was wrong, that they should remain in the oral domain and be passed on in the traditional ways; he was saddened that 'nobody sings "The Lass of Glenshee" right any more, since Harry Hibbs has it on the radio.'

With few exceptions, every singer thought that her or his own version was the 'right' version of any song, and that other singers must have gone astray somewhere along the line. We encountered women who had compiled their own songbooks, usually two or three scribblers bound together with ribbon or string, in which they wrote down the songs they loved 'so as not to be always forgetting the words.' These books are treasured and carefully kept clear of the children.

We noticed great differences in individual approaches to singing. Some singers had to be coaxed and coaxed, whereas with others you had to look smart to catch the first three words on tape. Some were lively and animated, using much gesturing; others assumed a stoical manner, becoming almost relieved when the song was ended; others closed their eyes and went into a private world; still others grabbed 'hold to' the nearest hands, pulling them back and forth as the song gained momentum. Two singers had to sit in their rocking chairs, which added an interesting dimension to the rhythm of their songs. One had the exasperating habit of smoking a pipe or chewing tobacco as he sang, which, since he had no teeth either, provided us with some unusual moments of transcription. A great many of the singers had the habit of speaking rather than singing the last few words of a song. We are told that this ritual was practised by ancient Greek singers to awaken their listeners from the ecstatic trance their songs were supposed to have induced.

While the majority of the singers we taped were getting on in years, there was a significant number of young people learning the songs and singing them whenever they had the opportunity. There seemed to be a kind of etiquette among some singers: a singer would usually have a repertoire which was known to everyone in the community; others would learn the songs, but when the original singer was present no amount of coaxing would get the song out of them. Sometimes the singer would invite them to 'help' with the song.

Just to write this brings to mind the bunches of young men lining the kitchen walls at Joe Brewer's in the Bight, singing the '*Thomas J. Hodder*'; the circle of grins that greeted Pius Power singing 'Charming Sally Ann'; the sound of the ocean and quiet ticking of the clock as Mrs Annie Green rocked and sang 'Thomas and Nancy.'

We remember the day when Uncle Mose Harris sang the song about the 'Limkin' and tried to teach us to play 'Amazing Grace' on the handsaw. There were the cups of tea and buns of hot bread spread with molasses we had down to Mr Frankie Nash's in Branch, and there was the night we stayed up until half-past four with Mrs Kate Wilson, amazed by the stories of her thirty years as a midwife on the island of Merasheen.

When we look at the songs we got from Mr Philip Foley, we cannot but wish that every reader could have been there to hear for themselves. The words on the page look bare and lifeless in comparison.

This book is dedicated to Mr Foley, Mose, Frankie, and Mrs Kate, who have all died since we started this collection. It is also dedicated to my father, Fred Best, who died before any of his songs could be recorded.

Anita Best
St John's 1983

Acknowledgments

We would like to extend thanks to those who have assisted in the preparation of this book, and especially to the following: Kelly Russell, Gerald Squires, Mrs Carla Furlong, Eric West, and Neil Murray for their letters of support when we applied for funding to complete the final manuscript;

Christine Earle and Jytte Selnø for proofreading the musical transcriptions and for their constant support throughout this project; the Canada Council Explorations Division for funding to collect most of the material; the Newfoundland and Labrador Arts Council and the 400th Anniversary Committee for funds to complete the final manuscript; Dr Kenneth Goldstein and Dr Wilf Wareham for their advice and information concerning some of the songs; Dr Herbert Halpert of Memorial University's Folklore Department for kindly letting us use some of the books in his library; Dr Gerald Thomas for advice and permission to use several Newfoundland French songs from his collection; Dr Aly O'Brien for his advice and help with the Irish Gaelic contained in some of the songs; Dr Harold Paddock of Memorial University's Linguistics Department for his advice concerning regional dialects of Newfoundland English; Philip Hiscock of Memorial University's Folklore Archive for his kind assistance; David Benson for advice on Newfoundland place names and history; David Panting for his assistance in proofreading the texts and transcribing songs; and Mr Ron Caplan for information concerning one of the songs in this collection.

Lastly, and most importantly, we are deeply grateful to the people of Newfoundland who so kindly welcomed us into their homes and sang us their songs.

Transcriber's Note

The singers represented in this book are of a unique and increasingly rare genre: in most cases they are people who have no musical training whatsoever, but have a vast and inexplicable, instinctive knowledge of music. Mostly, they have a story to tell, and the melodies they have absorbed from their elders since infancy are the vehicles of this expression.

I have transcribed this music not only to note the melodies but also to try and capture the unique singing style of each singer, including swoops and dips, irregular time changes, and the surprising grace note that appears from nowhere, quite out of the scale. This is the beauty of the songs of the people.

The only singers in this book who were not transcribed directly from tapes but from my memory are Philip and Bill Foley of Fogo Island. Their songs were too beautiful to exclude, and although I may not have done their highly embellished singing style justice, I believe the tunes to be accurate.

I would advise any singer not to be put off by all the irregularities. To sing these songs accurately is not to copy every grace note, but to sing from the heart, as these singers have done.

Pamela Morgan

Come and I Will Sing You

A Newfoundland Songbook

1 The Wreck of the *Annie Roberts*

Pius Power, Sr
Southeast Bight, 1977

Free time

O ye true born sons of New-found-land, come lis- ten un- to me and hear of the An- nie Ro- berts cut down when on the sea; a- bout two weeks a- -go to- day the An- nie she did sail on- -ly one man left out of her crew to tell the mournful tale.

2 O the *Annie Roberts* Sydney left being on a Thursday night
  With a crew of Newfoundlanders with spirits gay and bright;
  Filled up with coal for Lamaline that evening she did sail
  With her foresail and her mainsail reefed before a southwest gale.

3 She sailed along and all went well 'til on that fatal night
  When a steamer called the *Risenor* her port light hove in sight;
  Being on the *Annie* she bore down and terrified her crew
  And with a crash the schooner's side was quickly broke in two.

4 The commander of that iron ship have spun his vessel 'round
  But no sign of those missing men was nowhere to be found;
  Only one survivor from the wreck although he grabbed an oar –
  Got rescued by the steamer's crew and landed safe on shore.

5 O the commander of that iron ship have spun the vessel 'round
  But no sign of the missing men could anywhere be found;
  But one survivor from the wreck they carried him kind and well
  And landed him at Sydney, the sad tale there to tell.

3

6 The blow is hard for those at home and those that's left to mourn –
  Their mothers, wives, and sweethearts do wait for their return;
  They now sleeps in a watery grave, with loved ones left to weep
  For those brave hearty fishermen is buried in the deep.

The *Annie Roberts* was wrecked near Sydney, Nova Scotia, on 22 October 1913, en route to
Lamaline, Newfoundland.

Singer's key A♭

2 The *Annie Young*

Rosy Northcott
Ramea, 1977

Ye peo-ple all both great and small, I'll have you to un-der-
stand the per-ils of the o-cean when you are safe on
land; it's con-cer-ning of the An-nie Young, George
Hay-man in com-mand, and sev-en more bold and
stur-dy lads be-long to Fox Is-land.

2 On the twenty-fourth of August the truth I will relate,
  In nineteen hundred and thirty-five those poor men met their fate.
  They left their homes all full of joy, bound on the Labrador;
  Not thinking they would never see their home and friends no more.

3 The *Man Alone* was close alongside, George Warren in command;
  As they were keeping company about fifteen miles from land.
  The gale did blow so heavy, and it was growing night;
  They were forced to bring their schooners to, thought they'd ride it out all
    right.

4

4 But as the gale was raging, the seas were raging too;
   It was in the Gulf those boats did lie, and what more could they do.
   The *Man Alone* she rode it out, and they reached their homes all right;
   They lost sight of the light of the *Annie Young* about eleven o'clock that night.

5 What time those poor boys met their doom no tongue nor pen can tell;
   But we trust that they're in heaven, safe with the angels dwell.
   We know they fought hard for their lives, but it was all in vain;
   They sank below in a watery grave, and we'll never see them again.

6 The *Annie Young* was twenty-two tons and she was two years old;
   To look upon this noble boat she seemed to be very bold.
   The skipper of the *Man Alone* those words I heard him say:
   'That evening when the gale came on her mainsail tore away.'

7 The skipper was thirty-four years of age, left a wife and children three;
   We trust that they'll be looked upon and always happy be.
   We know he thought upon them when he saw he was doomed to die;
   To think of him lying in the deep, how mournful they would cry.

8 The second hand was a pleasant man, John McDonald was his name;
   He also left two children, we know he felt the same.
   To think about his orphans he was going to leave behind;
   We know he felt broken-hearted when they passed through his mind.

9 The other six were all single lads with hearts both brave and strong;
   Three of them were Coley boys, Fox Island did belong.
   John Warren and Bennie Hayman, the cook they had on board;
   And Johnnie Marks was the other lad that was called home by the Lord.

10 Those poor men all left parents who sadly for them weep;
   And talk about their loved ones that are lying in the deep.
   Their looks will never be forgot while relations do remain;
   Their places never will be filled in Fox Island again.

11 There are brothers and there are sisters who also for them weep;
   But they trust that God has guided them to a home of rest and sleep.
   We know it's hard to think about those eight young lives so fair;
   So little they thought when they left their home, their end it was so near.

12 So now my song is ended, I'll close it with regret.
   We may sail the ocean all around and dangers never meet;
   But we must all trust in the Lord and give to Him our love,
   That He may send us mercy from the heavens up above.

The *Annie Young* was lost in 1935. Her crew were all from Fox Island, off the Southwest Coast, and the vessel was owned by the firm of Penny in Ramea. Mrs Northcott's three cousins were lost in the storm; her husband, Mr Ken Northcott, was in the *Man Alone* that night. When the storm came on, the crew of the *Man Alone* passed alongside the *Annie Young*. The last words Mr Northcott heard from Mr McDonald were, 'The rain will be good for the women's gardens; it'll help them grow.' The storm grew fiercer and, from a distance, the *Man Alone* watched the *Annie*'s lights for five hours. Then her lights went out and she went down carrying eight seamen with her. The *Man Alone* barely survived herself and, almost a wreck, she drifted into Codroy. The men had been without food or water for thirty-seven hours.

The song was composed by Mr Walter Hayman, brother of one of the crew of the *Annie Young*.

3 Arthur

Annie Felix
Port au Port Peninsula, 1973

Vite

Ar-thur n'avait pas de ri- ches-se Il é- tait qu'un sim- ple ba- te
-lier Il s'en fut au châ- teau de la né- gres- se un cer-
-tain-(e) soir-(e) de juil- let D'un re- gard et d'un air si ten-dre
Ad- mir- a sa jeun-e beau-té mais(e) la mère de la né- gres-se
A dé-cou- vert tous leurs se- crets[1] mais(e) la mère de la né-
-gres- se A dé-cou- vert tous leurs se- crets.

2 La mère fut en rage et en colère
   Pour chasser Arthur hors de château
   Elle fut refârmer[2] la négresse
   Dans une[3] tour éloignée du château
   La nuit commençait à paraître
   Et les nuages à s'apaissir[4]
   A mit la tête par la fenêtre
   Pour voir son Arthur repartır. >*bis*

3 'Il est parti méchante mère
   Et pour moi y en est plus de bonheur
   C'est lui qu'accupait[5] ma mémoire
   C'est lui qui me disait toujours.
   'C'est toi négresse que j'adore
   A qui je donnerais ma vie
   Si tu reçois de mes nouvelles
   Pensez toujours à ton ami!'' ' >*bis*

4 Au bout de cinq ou six semaines
Chevalier venait la demander
Elle se tire de poche avec peine
Mouchoir[6] blanc tout en siglotant[7]
Dans son mouchoir on pouvait lire
Le nom d'Arthur était marqué
Mais elle avait fut[8] un soupir(e)
Mais ce soupir fut le dernier. > *bis*

1 Pronounced segret
2 Elle fit renfermer
3 Pronounced eune
4 Épaissir
5 Qui occupait
6 The syllable 'oir' is generally pronounced 'ouere'
7 Sanglotant
8 Avait fait

The song was collected by Gerald Thomas.

4 Aspell and Carter

Frankie Nash
Branch, 1976

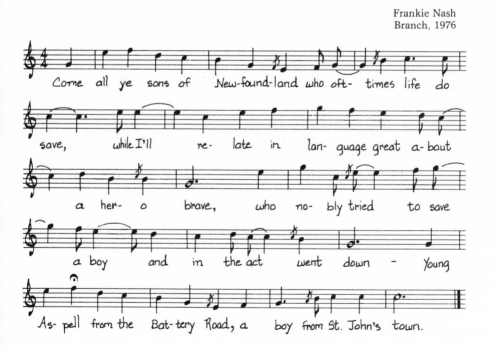

Come all ye sons of New-found-land who oft- times life do save, while I'll re- late in lan- guage great a- bout a her- o brave, who no- bly tried to save a boy and in the act went down – Young As- pell from the Bat- tery Road, a boy from St. John's town.

2 Young Carter that sad afternoon lighthearted left the town
   To take a bath, the day being warm, near Bennett's Grove went down;
   He divested of his clothing and boldly did leap in
   When soon the boys around the bank saw Carter could not swim.

3 He must have went beyond his depth, the overfall did pass
   Two youngsters sitting on the bank saw he was sinking fast.
   'O save me, save me,' Carter cried; the boys for aid did bawl
   Young Aspell strolling near the lake did hear the youngsters call.

4 He threw his coat upon the bank, rushed in the lake to try
   With outstretched arms a brave attempt to save the drowning boy.
   He caught his hand in death-like grasp and never reached the shore
   But held him in his dying grasp and sank to rise no more.

5 Young Aspell was a model youth both religious, good, and kind
   A fine and blooming clever lad his equals hard to find.
   Hard luck he had betimes, perhaps his manner did not show
   Just budding into manhood's bloom, it was a trying blow.

6 The prayer of many a sad, sad heart is gone to God on high
   For to receive the pure young soul of that good saintly boy,
   And fervent prayers from every home are offered, too, I'm sure
   For mercy on young Aspell's soul to Him who loves the poor.

This song concerns the drowning of John Aspell and F. Carter in July 1902, when Aspell attempted to save Carter's life at Quidi Vidi, a small outport community near St John's. The composer, Johnny Burke (1851-1930), was a well-known St John's balladeer who composed numerous popular songs including 'The Kelligrew's Soiree' and 'The Trinity Cake.' For a biography of Johnny Burke, see James D. Higgins, *The Bard of Prescott Street* (St John's 1970), available at the Centre for Newfoundland Studies, Queen Elizabeth II Library, Memorial University.

Singer's key A^b

5 The August Gale (A)

Ray Hepditch and others
Southeast Bight, 1976

On the twen-ty-fifth of Au-gust the gale be-gan to rise, which left so man-y or-phans and took so man-y lives; left there to stay for their last day, their friends to see no-more, for the o-cean wave it rolled that day like it ne-ver rolled be-fore.

2 John Follett in his little boat about ten tons or more,
Was anchored on the fishing ground about twelve miles from the shore;
And when the gale begun to rise, they run to the nearest port,
But a heavy sea rolled over them and capsized their little boat.

3 John Follett and one of his sons clung to the wreck that day,
For eight long hours they drifted, exposed to wind and sea;
God spared the lives of those poor boys, all for to tell the tale,
But his eldest son got drownded in that great August gale.

4 Danny Cheeseman from Rushoon also went down that day,
The boat was passed with her two spars gone about half-ways in the bay;
To think on what they suffered, a stone would heave a sigh;
There were three men clinging to the wreck when Harris passed her by.

5 He tried his best to save them but the boat she did misstay,
And with aching hearts they were forced to part and run before wind and sea;
He done his whole endeavour, 'twas all that he could do;
May the Lord have mercy on the souls of Dan Cheeseman and his crew.

6 Another schooner branded new, built up in Mortier Bay,
Commanded by John Locklin from Red Harbour sailed away;
As she was anchored on Cape ground to the west'ard of the light,
She had a dory gone astray that dark and stormy night.

7 The *Annie* from Fox Harbour also went down that day,
   With seven hearty fishermen, no more to plough the sea;
   And all of them being married men, which made the loss run high,
   Excepting one, the skipper's son, he was a single boy.

8 There's six young widows left to mourn, I know them all quite well,
   With children small, no help at all to bear their troubles well;
   If God Himself will lend a hand and look down on them, I hope,
   Leaving widows and orphans for to mourn – it was a dreadful stroke.

The August Gale (B)

Frankie Nash
Branch, 1976

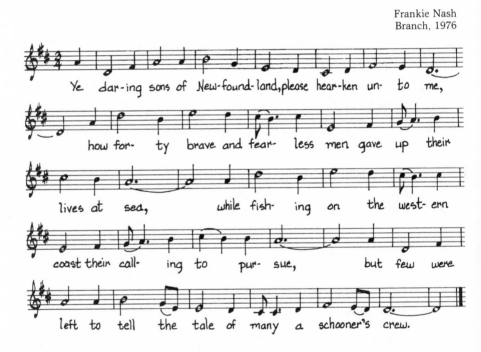

Ye dar-ing sons of New-found-land, please hear-ken un-to me,
how for-ty brave and fear-less men gave up their
lives at sea, while fish-ing on the west-ern
coast their call-ing to pur-sue, but few were
left to tell the tale of many a schooner's crew.

2 They left homes with happy hearts all full of mirth and glee,
   Not thinking as they sailed that morn no more their homes to see;
   No more to see their children dear, their kind and loving wives;
   For in that storm on Thursday morn those brave men lost their lives.

3 The wind with fury it did blow that fatal Thursday morn,
   They reefed their mainsail and their jib for to ride out the storm;
   But all in vain their tiny craft the fury could not stand,
   And these brave heroes lost their lives while trying to make the land.

4 The winds did blow with fearful force and no let up that day
As all the boats were on the ground around Placentia Bay;
Came beating home in that wild storm, the sea rolled mountains high,
And those brave souls they saw no hope, gave up their lives to die.

5 It is a hard and a trying blow for those that's left to weep;
The sole provider of their homes now sleeps beneath the deep.
Their wives and orphans left to mourn, their widows' only son
Are also numbered with the dead, God's will it must be done.

6 So let us pray for those away who on the sea must roam
And guard them in their tiny craft and send them safe at home;
And put your trust in Providence and trust to Him on high,
To send those brave ones home again and fill our hearts with joy.

7 All things do happen for the best and when they're called away,
The brave lads on the ocean, out in the storm that day;
We hope they'll see a better land from sorrow and from care
In that bright land above us all, its splendour for to share.

In August 1935, Placentia Bay was hit by a severe storm known as the August Gale which claimed the lives of forty fishermen. The Harris mentioned in the fourth stanza of the first version is the well-known Captain James Harris.

Aunt Carrie Brennan related how the morning following the storm, she and her husband, Mr Ned Brennan, walked out to the beach near their home in Ship Cove and saw the wreckage of a ship. A man was seen strapped to the ship's rigging which was rising and falling with the motion of the waves. It was thought he might still be alive, but he was found dead when Mr Brennan rowed out and cut him down. The body was that of Captain John Locklin. The bodies of the other men gradually drifted to shore, and their families were notified accordingly. A boy's kitbag washed up on the beach – the clothes within all neatly folded, and his small mouth-organ nestled among the clothing. The bag bore the name of Joshua Barrett, Woody Island, Placentia Bay. He and another man had gone astray in a dory the night before.

The first version was composed by Billy Wilson of Merasheen Island, Placentia Bay, and the second is attributed to the penmanship of Johnny Burke.

6 The Banks of Sweet Dundee

Moses Harris
Lethbridge, 1976

It's of a far- mer's daugh- ter, so beau- ti- ful I'm
told; her par- ents died and leaved her a
large sum of gold. She lived with her rich un-cle,
was the cause of all her woe, and soon you'll
hear this mai- den fair that proved his o- ver- throw.

2 Her uncle had a ploughboy who Mary loved quite well,
Down in her uncle's garden fond tales of love did tell;
There dwelled a wealthy squire who Mary came to see,
But still she loved her ploughboy on the banks of sweet Dundee.

3 Her uncle and the squire rode out on one fine day:
'Young Willie he's in favour,' her uncle he did say,
'And this is my intention, to tie him to a tree
And then to bribe a press-gang on the banks of sweet Dundee.'

4 Her uncle rose one morning, straightway to her he came
And knocking on her bedroom door, those words to her did say:
'Arise, arise my fair pretty maid, for a lady you will be;
The squire is now a-waiting for you on the banks of sweet Dundee.'

5 'I care not for your lords or squires, your dukes nor earls likewise –
My Willie's eyes appears to me like diamonds in the skies.'
'Be gone undaunted fair maid, unhappy you will be,
For I will banish Willie from the banks of sweet Dundee.'

6 The press-gang came to Willie when he was all alone,
He boldly fought for liberty, but there was six to one;
The blood did flow in torrents: 'Pray kill me now,' said he,
'For I will die for Mary on the banks of sweet Dundee.'

7 As Mary was a-walking, lamenting for her love
She meet the wealthy squire down in her uncle's grove.
'Stand off! Stand off!' cried Mary, 'Undaunted will I be,
'Twas you that drove the lad I love from the banks of sweet Dundee.'

8 He throwed his arms around her and he tried to throw her down –
Two pistols and a sword she saw beneath his morning gown;
She took the weapons from him, and the sword he used so free,
She fired and shot the squire on the banks of sweet Dundee.

9 Her uncle overheard the noise and hastened to the sound,
Saying: 'Since you shot the squire, I'll give you your death wound';
'Stand off! Stand off!' cried Mary, 'Undaunted will I be.'
The trigger drew, her uncle slew on the banks of sweet Dundee.

10 The doctor he was sent for and a man of perfect skill,
And likewise a lawyer for him to sign his will –
His gold he willed to Mary, who fought so manfully
And he closed his eyes, no more to rise on the banks of sweet Dundee.

Moses Harris is the man's name, but his nickname or the name he was always called by is Uncle Mose. This is one of the first songs I heard him sing, if not the first. He said it was one of his favourite songs – Uncle Mose knew so many that it must have been only one among countless favourites. He told me one time that if he heard a song just once he 'had it' and could sing it back to the person who sang it to him.

MERCER 96

7 Betsy Beauty

Lillian Pittman
Placentia, 1975

Bet- sy beau- ty so bright and fair, who
late- ly came from Der- by- shire, a
ser- ving maid she proved to be to a
rich old la- dy of high de- gree.

2 This lady had but one only son
Whose heart by women had never been won,
But Betsy Beauty so bright and fair
Drew Johnny's heart into a snare.

3 He went one night, as you soon shall find,
And thus began to relieve his mind
Saying: 'Betsy, I love you as I love my life
And I do intend to make you my wife.

4 His mother in the next bedroom lay,
And hearing what her dear son did say
Resolved she was in her own mind
To flusterate her own son's designs.

5 Early next morning his mother arose
Saying: 'Get up Betsy, put on your clothes;
Out of this town now you must go
To wait on me one day or two.'

6 Now Betsy arose, put on her clothes
And away with her mistress she did go.
Saying: 'There's a ship lies in this town,
And to Virginia, Betsy you're bound.'

7 Quite late that night his mother returned.
'B'right well returned, dear mother,' said he,
'B'right well returned, dear mother,' he said,
'But where is Betsy, your waiting maid?'

8 'O son, dear son, I would rather see
You in your grave than to wed Betsy;
To equal Betsy along with me
This sore disgrace I don't wish to see.'

9 'O mother dear, you are most unkind
You have ruined the soul and body of mine;
And your desire you soon shall have
When I am in my silent grave.'

10 Now Johnny took to his lovesick bed;
The thoughts of Betsy ran in his head.
In slumbering dreams he would sigh and say:
'O charming Betsy, so far away!'

11 They sent for doctors both far and near,
But no relief could he find there.
In slumbering dreams he would sigh and cry:
'O charming Betsy, for you I'll die!'

12 When his mother saw her son was dead,
She wrang her hands and she tore her head,
Saying: 'If love could bring life back again
I would send for Betsy far o'er the main.'

Lillian Pittman learned this song from family tradition. It was popular with the women in
Merasheen who would get together at wedding and garden parties and sing it in unison.
There would usually be one lead singer to establish the key.

8 The Blow below the Belt

Anthony Ward
St John's, 1983

I'm sit- ting here on Har- vey's pier in the ci- ty of St.
John's; I'm think- ing back on South-east Bight, the
place where I was born; I'm think- ing back on Pla-
-cen- tia Bay, where all our peo- ple left, af- ter
sign- ing up that Govern-ment plan, the blow be- low the belt.

2 'Twas in the year of 'sixty-six, the date I won't forget.
The Government Plan was sent around, I can see that paper yet,
'Sign it if you want to, or reject it if you like,
The rules and regulations they're there in black and white.

3 Two hundred for each person, a thousand to freeze your land,
Your house and property's still your own – you may sell it if you can.'
Some beautiful homes were left behind for what else could we do?
If you asked someone to buy your home, he'd say: 'We're leaving, too.'

4 Smallwood he got on the air, each word he spoke seemed great:
'Haul up your punts and dories! Destroy your stage and flake!
I'm moving you away from here, employment sure you'll find,
And you won't regret the day you left those outports far behind.'

5 When fifty percent of the people the Government Plan did sign
The other fifty had no choice 'twas go or be left behind;
We moved in all directions all around our native coast,
And bid good-bye to our home-sweet-homes, the places we cherished most.

6 After we resettled, everything seemed pretty odd –
Us independent fishermen, we could not find a job.
But when elections rolled around, we showed Joey how we felt,
We dropped him in his corner and gave Frank Moores the belt!

15

7 There's one man's name I'll mention, I'm sure that he won't mind,
   That gentleman's name is Pius Power, he's a real good friend of mine –
   He moved from Clattice Harbour back to the place I left;
   He would not sign that dotted line, that blow below the belt.

8 He's an independent fisherman, everything he got, he owns,
   Fishing gear of many kinds – a schooner twenty tons.
   He's as friendly a chap as ever you met, and he'll tell you how he felt,
   Why he would not sign the dotted line, the blow below the belt.

9 Now to conclude and finish, I'm still on Harvey's Pier
   A-gazing through the Narrows o'er the sleepy ocean near.
   I'm an employee at the Waterford, I was lucky, sure, myself,
   That I didn't end up a patient from the blow below the belt.

This song's lyrics were written by Anthony Ward, originally of Southeast Bight. Anthony is a prolific songwriter, though he usually leaves it up to somebody else to compose the tune; in this case, the composer was Dave Panting.

The Resettlement Program was carried out in Newfoundland during Joseph Smallwood's government from the 1950s to the early 1970s. Its aim was to relocate fishermen and their families from coastal communities to larger centres where they would find better job opportunities and public facilities such as hospitals and schools. Many of these people were introduced to social assistance for the first time in their lives since the promised jobs were fictional. Placentia Bay was particularly hard-struck. When the smoke had finally cleared over three hundred communities had been completely closed down and those that remained were tombstones marking the passing of a large and noble part of our history.

The Waterford Hospital is a mental health institution in St John's.

9 The *Blue Wave*

John (Jack) Lushman, Sr
Ramea, 1977

Come all ye men that work on land, for lit-tle do you know what we poor fish-er-men en-dure when the stor-my winds do blow; 'twas Feb-ru-ar-y in 'fif-ty-nine, a date I re-mem-ber well, when some brave lads were called a-way out in that hea-vy gale.

2 We sailed away from Burgeo, it was on a Sunday morn,
The temperature reading zero as we ran before a storm.
Bill Vardy was our skipper's name, the *Triton* was our boat;
Our crew was all from Newfoundland, there's no better bunch afloat.

3 We fished around those Grand Banks five or six days or more,
When a heavy storm it did arise as we headed for the shore.
It wasn't very long afterwards the news we all did know,
A sea struck the *Cape Dolphin* and she was sinking slow.

4 'Fore ten on Monday morning we received a distress shout,
Coming from the *Blue Wave* saying that she was hove out;
We tried to run back to her but nothing would she stand.
We brought her to the wind again and we shaped her for the land.

5 Our captain then gave orders the ice for to beat off.
We beat a load down on her deck, and we beat it from aloft.
We kept beating away the ice, our hearts were filled with fear;
Our captain then gave orders again our lifeboats to keep clear.

6 Then aeroplanes were soon despatched to search the ocean 'round,
But no sign of their missing boat was anywhere to be found.
A gale of wind was blowing then, while the seas rose mountains high;
The search it was abandoned, and the planes did homeward fly.

7 To you people of Grand Bank and Fortune I send my deepest sympathy;
   Put your trust in God above while toiling on the sea.
   Don't fret nor mourn for those brave lads that have been called away;
   I know you'll meet in heaven above upon that judgment day.

8 Now to conclude and finish, I think I have done well.
   My name and my birthplace I'm going for to tell;
   Grey River is my native home, Jack Lushman is my name
   And I sailed with Captain Vardy from Burgeo, Newfoundland.

In February 1959 the *Blue Wave*, with a crew from Grand Bank and Fortune, was struck by a heavy storm and left to the mercy of the waves. The *Triton* from Burgeo was sent to her aid, but under such severe and hazardous conditions there was nothing the crew could do. The *Cape Dolphin* mentioned in the song was also in distress, but her crew were rescued and brought safe to land.

   I recorded this song from the composer, Mr John Lushman, Sr. He told me he spent twenty-eight years on the sea, but he is glad to be a landsman once again.

10 Bold Hawke

Ernest Barter
Ramea, 1977

The eigh-teenth day of De-cem-ber last in Tor-bay we did lay — Bold Hawke he hois-ted his flag my boys, and soon got un-der way; the hea-vens may pro--tect us with a sweet and pleas-ant breeze, we hois-ted up her top-sail and soon crossed o-ver the waves.

2 The twenty-eighth of that same month the weather being clear –
  Bold Hawke he spied five lofty ships to the leeward of us lay;
  Bold Hawke himself he mounted up in the lofty air,
  His wings he spread so large my boys, and right after them did steer.

3 The first broadside we gave to them we hit one on a cream –
  'Twas such a glorious broadside, the likes was seldom seen;
  We gave to them another like thunder loud did roar,
  We sunk the French so fast my boys, all on their native shore.

4 To see the *Lily* of France my boys, see how she's sinking down –
  With many a heavy sigh on board, with many a heavy wound;
  The *Rising Sun* we burneth and the French *Glory* likewise,
  We sunk the *Lily* of France my boys, and the rest we made our prize.

5 So now the wars are over, we'll fill the sparkling bowl –
  It's while we're on the sea or land, our enemies we'll control;
  Here's luck to our commander both loyal, just, and true
  Likewise Sir Edward Hawke my boys, and the *Royal George*'s crew.

This song commemorates Sir Edward Hawke's defeat of the Brest fleet in November 1759, at Quiberon Bay on the coast of France. This battle was recorded in British history as one of the greatest naval victories of all time. The song appeared in a collection of broadsheet ballads called *Real Sailor Songs*, collected and edited by John Aston (1891), with an introduction by A.L. Lloyd (1973). Lloyd says that the author of 'Hawke's Engagement,' as it is known in that collection, was most likely someone aboard the flagship *Royal George*.

11 Bold Larkin

Ray Hepditch and others
Southeast Bight, 1975

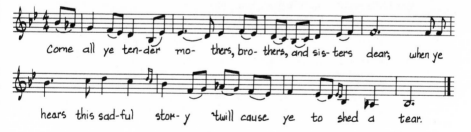

Come all ye ten-der mo-thers, bro-thers, and sis-ters dear, when ye hears this sad-ful stor-y 'twill cause ye to shed a tear.

2 If it's any offence please stop my hand, by you I'll be advised –
  I means to state what did take place in the year of 'sixty-five.

3 O Monday being our forty-eighth tossed on the raging main –
  One pound of bread on board of us each man for to maintain.

4 Being on a Tuesday morn, April the twenty-fourth,
  Neptune was on board of us and loudly did he roar.

5 'No land, no light,' Bold Larkin cries, 'No land lies in our view!
   For the daylight is approaching and for it we will heave to.'

6 And when the daylight cleared away, Cape Spear we chanced to spy;
   'Heave out, heave out my lively lads, to get her in we'll try.'

7 Two youths to loosen our fore-course, his orders to obey –
   When one of these poor fellows fell out off Cape Spear that day.

8 Exactly at the time he fell, she was taking eight and a half from the reel;
   And instantly our helmsman down starboard swung the wheel.

9 Our main yards swung, our good ship come, and a boat was lowered by
      hand –
   Eight minutes and a half from the time he fell 'til the boat was afloat and
      manned.

10 Like hearty tars to save him they rowed with all their skill –
   The breakers white all 'round them foamed, and their boat began to fill.

11 God help him poor fellow, he soon went out of sight –
   Neptune on board of us combined and roared with all his might.

12 His time was come, his glass was run, his Maker to go see –
   I hope that the Almighty will receive him joyfully.

13 When we came through the Narrows, the wind was veering down,
   We hoist our colours half-mast high to beat her up the town.

14 To see his agèd father as we hauled to the pier;
   Big drops of tears rolling down his cheeks, and tearing of his hair.

15 He cries out broken-hearted: 'Where did you leave my child?'
   His tender mother when she is told will certainly go wild.

16 'O father dear, don't blame us for the losing of your son –
   Mother do not weep for him but pray for him that's gone.'

17 Your prayer shall be accepted and answered in great fame –
   And the soul of Ambrose Sheehan, may it rest in peace, AMEN.

Aunt Carrie Brennan is a most careful singer to whom the lyrics of a song are of the
utmost importance. She told us that in her rendition of this song she changed a word here
and there to preserve the dignity of the event. One such change occurs in stanza 15 – she
substituted 'could not be reconciled' for 'will certainly go wild.' The version we have
included was sung by a group of young fishermen from Southeast Bight, Placentia Bay, one
fall night in 1975. The song is a great favourite in that area, but is known by only a few
singers, perhaps because, as Ray Hepditch said, 'It's a song you have to start out right or
you'll get nowhere with it.'
   'Bold Larkin,' also known as 'The Loss of Andrew Sheehan,' was composed by John
Grace. Sheehan was a native of St John's. In a version of the song printed in Murphy's
Songs Their Fathers Sung, the date of the event is '55 and not '65 as in our version. Larkin is
also written as Harkin in Murphy's book.

MERCER 148

12 Bonny Blue-eyed Jane

Philip Foley
Tilting, 1979

Slow and sad, with feeling

Here's a- dieu un- to my na- tive home that I shall see no more, with love my thoughts will turn to thee when on a for- eign shore; fare- well to friends and par- ents dear, from you I'll part in pain, like- wise to you my bloom- ing girl, my bon-ny blue-eyed Jane.

2 When I am absent from your side out on the lone blue sea,
Your image bright unto my mind will ever foremost be
To cheer me in my lonely watch until I see again
The form of her I love so well, my bonny blue-eyed Jane.

3 When far beneath the sunny skies in foreign lands I roam,
Powerless will their beauty be to win my love from home;
Though I may meet in friendship with the girls from sunny Spain,
They will not win my love from you, my bonny blue-eyed Jane.

4 O were I born of noble blood with wealth at my command,
I'd share it all with her I love that girl so fair and grand.
The pearls from the ocean depths devoid of spot or stain
Would not enhance the beauty of my bonny blue-eyed Jane.

5 And if kind fortune should decree that riches I should find,
With loving haste I'd return to her the girl I left behind –
Across the deep and changeful seas from roving I'd refrain
And marry her I love so well, my bonny blue-eyed Jane.

This lovely immigrant song is rarely sung in Newfoundland. Its strong Irish flavour and poetic language were well suited to Mr Foley's style of singing.

13 Brave Marin

Anita Best
St John's, 1983

Slowly

'Bra-ve ma-rin re-vient de guer-re, tout mal chaus-sé, tout mal vê-tu; bra-ve ma-rin d'où re-viens-tu?'

2 'Madame, je reviens de guerre.
Que l'on m'apporte du vin blanc,
Que le marin boive en passant.'

3 'Brave marin se mit à boire,
Se mit à rire et à chanter,
Et la belle hôtesse à pleurer.'

4 'Ah, qu'avez-vous, ma belle hôtesse?
Regrettez-vous votre vin blanc
Que le marin boit en passant?'

5 'C'est pas le vin que je regrette,
Mais les soucis de mon mari
Et je crois bien que vous êtes lui.'

6 'Taisez-vous ma belle hôtesse!
Vous avez donc trois beaux enfants,
Ma femme et moi, nous n'avons q'un.'

7 'Je t'en reçu de fausses lettres
Que vous étiez mort, enterré,
Et je me suis remariée.'

8 Brave marin vida son verre
Mit sur la table pièces d'argent
Et retourna au régiment.

While visiting Cape St Georges in the late 1960s, I learned this song from a woman who had spent most of her life in St Pierre et Miquelon. It dates from the time of the wars of Louis XIV (the late 1600s) and was very popular in the southwest of France. A.B.

22

14 The Brule Boys

Mary (Min) Caul
Arnold's Cove, 1977

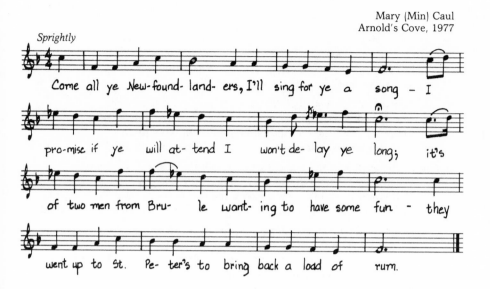

Sprightly

Come all ye New-found-land-ers, I'll sing for ye a song – I pro-mise if ye will at-tend I won't de-lay ye long; it's of two men from Bru- le want-ing to have some fun – they went up to St. Pe-ter's to bring back a load of rum.

2 The day it being a fine one and the sun was shining bright,
When those two men from Brule arrived there just at night;
They took on board a heavy stock and then the wind veered down –
They then set sail for Brule, leaving St Peter's town.

3 They runned her for St Lawrence and the sky looked kind of black.
Our skipper said: 'Now we'll go in where we can take a nap.'
We anchored 'round the point of the beach and put their line ashore;
Our skipper said: 'Now we can sleep while the wind and sea do roar.'

4 That night the storm kept raging, but we came through all right –
And when the water smoothened down 'twas then we put her out;
Being late up in the evening, the sky looked kind of clear,
But very shortly after, the wind began to veer.

5 The wind came from the east'ard, and the sky fell thick with snow;
And now the storm is raging, he says: 'Where can we go?
We have no compass for a guide, no means to make a light.'
The waters still washed over them on that cold winter's night.

6 'We must give up and pray to God,' our skipper he did say,
'For we can't live no longer, for this is our last day!'
They thought of friends and loved ones whom they had left on shore,
And took each other by the hand to part forevermore.

7 O who can tell the feeling of those two Brule men,
Tossed on the stormy ocean with nothing to comfort them;
The blood was frozen in their veins, the salt tears in their eyes –
They raised their eyes to heaven above, and they muttered mournful cries.

8 They drifted before wind and sea all that long cruel night –
And when the daylight cleared away, no land or strand in sight.
But very shortly after, a vessel hove in sight –
The captain's name was Harvey, was out that long winter's night.

9 When Harvey saw them coming, he called: 'All hands on deck –
O come and look to wind'ard and see that little jack.
Have we no means of saving them?'. he said unto his crew;
'Get ropes and lifeboats ready, and we'll see what we can do.'

10 Those men got near that vessel, hailing with all their might,
Crying: 'Save us, captain, save us – do try to save our lives!'
There was no time for talking, he told them what to do –
'Just run around our quarter, and then heave her head to.'

11 In the shelter of the vessel drifted this little jack.
When they got hold of those two men, they dragged them in on deck,
And took them to the cabin where they were treated kind –
And placed them by a hard-coal fire and gave them boiled claret wine.

12 Now Harvey he gave orders, unto his men did say:
'The wind is on the drop, me boys, so get her underway –
Go trim your canvas by the wind and then we'll reef her down.'
And on the following evening we arrived at Marystown.

13 O telegrams were soon dispatched unto their friends and wives,
And said how Harvey picked them up and saved their precious lives;
Theirselves will tell the story on some cold winter's night,
In praise of Captain Harvey who saved their precious lives.

14 It was the hand of Providence that brought him in this bay,
And saved those men from Brule, all for a longer day;
They thought their time had come to go their friends to see no more,
And now they're safely landed once more on Brule shore.

15 Before that I do finish, for Harvey I must say:
'May the great God protect him while sailing on the sea –
And grant him all the pleasure in every port he'll find,
For saving those two Brule men and acting very kind.'

16 Come all ye men from Brule, I'll have ye to beware –
Don't ye go to St Peter's 'til the springtime of the year;
While winter storms are raging I'm afraid you'll get a fright,
For Harvey won't be always there waiting to save your life!

Brule, a community on Merasheen Island in Placentia Bay, was one of the prime smuggling areas for the St Pierre rum-running operation. The two lads in the song were on such a venture when caught in a severe storm. Much of the smuggling was done between 1850 and 1950. However, this song takes place in the early 1900s.

The Buck Goat Song

15 The Buck Goat Song

Moses Harris
Lethbridge, 1977

Come lis-ten I'll tell youse a sto-ry, I
can't think of no o-ther way; I'll
tell you how I took a beat-ing out
dig-ging po-ta-toes one day.

2 I was digging away at potatoes,
   When the nanny goat scenes they did pour;
   If there was one there's a thousand,
   Oh boys, how I cursed and I swore.

3 Then out in the middle of the field,
   Old billy he started to sway;
   And the perfume he had on 'twas rotten,
   You could smell it for miles away.

4 Then I lost all my patience,
   And a picket I tore from the fence;
   I started to drive out the nannies,
   When something hit me in the pants.

5 The first place that old billy landed me,
   I'm sorry I can't name the place;
   He knocked me down in the gravel,
   And he rubbed his old nose in my face.

6 His arms they got caught in my sweater,
   And then I started to pray;
   'Oh God, up in heaven, have mercy,
   I'm fighting with no referee.'

7 Now if you'll excuse my bad language,
   I'm trying to keep back the oaths;
   I tell you that I'm not religious,
   For I lost it out there on the goats.

8 Now Wilcox he thinks he's a boxer,
   Joe Louis he thinks he's just swell;
   But they'd all lose their bout in a hurry,
   If they had to fight that old bill.

This comical ditty was written by Mr Edmund Chaffey of Musgravetown, Bonavista Bay. It was requested several times when Mr Harris performed at the Good Entertainment Festival, a one-time folk festival held in St John's in 1977. The last time he sang it at the festival, he asked that anyone present in the audience from Musgravetown please pass it along to Edmund Chaffey that he had sung his song.

16 Caroline from Edinboro (Edinburgh) Town

Mick Keough
Plate Cove, 1976

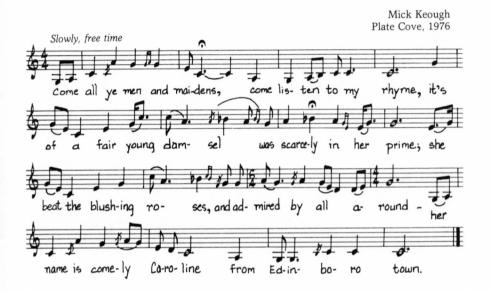

Slowly, free time

Come all ye men and mai-dens, come lis- ten to my rhyme, it's of a fair young dam- sel was scarce-ly in her prime; she beat the blush-ing ro- ses, and ad- mired by all a- round - her name is come-ly Ca-ro- line from Ed-in- bo- ro town.

2 Young Henry was an Highlandman, a-courting her he came,
   And when her parents came to know they did not like the same;
   Enticed by young Henry she put on another gown
   And away went comely Caroline from Edinboro town.

3 Over hills and lofty mountains together they did roam
   Until they reached London far from her happy home;
   She says: 'My dearest Henry, if ever on me you'll frown
   You'll break the heart of Caroline from Edinboro town.'

4 They were not at London the space of a half a year,
   When cruel, hard-hearted Henry, he proved to her severe;
   He says: 'My dearest Caroline, your parents on me did frown
   So beg your way without delay to Edinboro town.'

27

5 Out on the plain this maid did go, all to the world exposed –
Going in the woods to each such fruit as on the bushes grow;
Some of the people pitied her and more on her did frown
And more did say: 'Why did you stray from Edinboro town?'

6 Down by a lofty spreading oak this maid kneeled down to cry,
A-viewing of the gallant fleet as they go passing by;
She gave three screams for Henry, and threw her body down,
Saying: 'Here I lie, lament, and die, from Edinboro town.'

7 A note, likewise her bonnet, she left upon the shore
With a lock of hair, and these words: 'I am no more;
I'm in the deep, lying fast asleep, while fish are watching 'round
Once comely young Caroline from Edinboro town.'

The last verse of this lovely song is from the reciting of Mr Felix Morey of Bonavista, from whom I first heard it. However, Mr Morey did not provide a tune so I have used Mr Mick Keough's version. Both texts do not vary a great deal, and so I did not print the two variants.

Singer's key A♭

Carroll Bán

17 Carroll Bán

Carrie Brennan
Ship Cove, 1978

Compassionately

'Twas in the town of Wex-ford they sen-tenced him to die, 'twas in the town of Wex-ford they built a gal-lows high; and there one sun-ny morn-ing while beamed a plea-sant dawn, up-on that cur-sèd gib-bet they hung my Car-roll Bán.

2 O he was true and loyal, O he was proud and fair,
And only nineteen summers shone on his golden hair;
And when his gallant brothers had grasped the pike in hand,
Where the green flag streamed the fairest, he stood for his native land.

3 I saw him cross the heather with his bold company,
And from the rising hillside he waved his hand to me;
Then on my wild heart settled a load of woe and pain,
Mo bhrón it's throbbing told me we'd never meet again.

4 He fought the Saxon foemen by Slaney's glancing wave,
But brutal strength o'erpowered the gallant and the brave;
And in the fight which followed, that day of misery,
Sore wounded he was taken my Carroll bán mo chroí.

5 O fhíor ghéar that ever I saw the dreadful sight,
His locks all damply hanging and his cheeks a deadly white.
What wonder if my ringlets would change from dark to grey,
Or if the blessèd hand of God would take my life away.

6 The meadow path is lonely, and the hearth is cold and dim,
And the silent churchyard blossom blooms softly over him;
And my heart that's ever sobbing for the calm rest coming on,
With its weary pulse lies sleeping beside my Carroll bán.

'Carroll Bán' was written by John Keegan Casey (Leo), (1846-70), an Irish patriot, concerning the 1798 Wexford Rebellion, one of the many uprisings in which the Irish fought against the oppression and injustice inflicted upon them by their more powerful English neighbours. Casey wrote many popular songs including 'The Rising of the Moon' and 'Máire My Girl.' He died at the age of twenty-three as a result of imprisonment for his involvement in the Fenian Brotherhood.

The song contains several Irish Gaelic words perfectly enunciated by Aunt Carrie, even though she did not know their meaning. 'Mo chroí' (machree) means 'my love' or 'my heart'; 'mo bhrón' (mavrone or marone) means 'o my sorrow'; and 'fhíor ghéar' (fear gear) is an expression of intense grief or pain. 'Bán' means fair and is often written in English as 'bawn,' indicating its pronunciation.

Singer's key A♭

18 The Champion of Court Hill

Val Ryan
St John's, 1975

Slowly, free time

In smil-ing June when ro-ses bloom and the Warbler cheers the grove, by a bab-bling brook my way I took quite care-less-ly to roam; I met with White, my heart's de-light, saying why is it you're a-lone? O the day being fine, if you're in-clined, o a-long with me to roam.'

2 'I am sorry but I can't accept your invitation now,
For my maw she will be harsh at me, or no pastime she'll allow.'
'Your maw won't know where we will go, sure let us try our skill,
We will walk awhile, we will sit and smile, convenient to Court Hill.'

3 O she gave consent, 'twas on we went on our discourse along –
'Twas manys a time he said to me: 'No one I love but thee.'
But now he's gone and wed to one by the name of Belle Madel,
And I'm left, poor Kate, in that sad state, heart-broken on Court Hill.

4 O you ladies all both great and small, o a warning take by me,
Don't never depend on any young man until the knot is tied;
For if you do you'll surely rue, like me you'll cry your fill –
For I am ruined right, by Willie White, the champion of Court Hill.

Several people have suggested to me that the song may be referring to Coote Hill in Ireland. The song certainly has an Irish flavour. Val learned it from Clem Bonia of North Harbour, St Mary's Bay (where Val is originally from). There is a part he can't remember, and therefore I have had to rearrange a couple of the lines so that the verses conform to the tune.

Singer's key B♭m

19 Charming Blue-eyed Mary

Dorman Ralph
St John's, 1977

2 'Where are you going my fair pretty maid, where are you going so early?'
'I'm going milking, kind sir,' said she, 'from that on to my dairy.'

3 'Must[1] I come too my fair pretty maid, must I come, too, so early?'
'Do as you wish, young man,' she cried, 'for charming blue-eyed Mary.'

4 They walked and talked over hills and fields, where skylarks they were singing
Until they came to some mossy banks where primroses they were blooming.

5 They both sat down on the mossy banks where they knew no one could hear them;
It was there he kissed the rosy lips of charming blue-eyed Mary.

6 'And since you got the will of me, I pray young man don't leave me;
If I should prove a child by thee, my parents they would scorn me.'

7 Kisses so sweet he gave to her, just as those words were spoken
And a diamond ring he gave to her saying: 'Take this as a token.'

8 'For I must be gone by the break of dawn, our ship she do sail early;
And it's now I'll bid a long farewell to charming blue-eyed Mary.'

9 As six long months being gone and past, no letter came to Mary
Which caused her to view her diamond ring as she sat in her dairy.

10 But eight long months being gone and past she saw her true love Jimmy
Saying: 'It's now I'm come to wed at last young charming blue-eyed Mary.'

11 'Will you forsake your houses and land, your cattle, and your dairy
All for to be a captain's bride?' 'I will,' cried blue-eyed Mary.

12 'I will forsake my houses and land, my cattle and my dairy
All for to sail far o'er the main, I will,' cried blue-eyed Mary.

1 This is an older dialect form of must used in question form and meaning may or shall.

Dr Kenneth Goldstein writes of this song in *The Livyere:* 'Though its theme of true love
rewarded is not uncommon in folksong, this delightful ballad is rare indeed. The oldest
version we know is from a songsheet or broadside printed by J. Catnach in London in the
early nineteenth century.' Dorman learned many of his songs from his family and relatives
– this one he learned from his Aunt Dorcas Ralph, White Bay.

20 Charming Sally Ann

Pius Power, Sr
Southeast Bight, 1980

With spirit

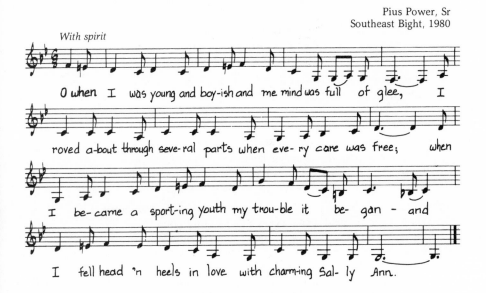

O when I was young and boy-ish and me mind was full of glee, I
roved a-bout through seve-ral parts when eve-ry care was free; when
I be-came a sport-ing youth my trou-ble it be-gan – and
I fell head 'n heels in love with charm-ing Sal-ly Ann.

2 O the first time that I met her it being to a good ol' spree –
Sometimes I looked at Sally Ann, each time she winked at me;
And when I looked at Sally I was crazy as a span!
I was crazy as a bed-bug for my charming Sally Ann.

3 O the next time that I met her it was to her father's door –
I conversed with her mother for a full long hour or more;
When up speaks Sally's mother saying: 'I'll do what I can
For to bring you on condolence with my daughter Sally Ann.'

4 O I went up next evening the old folks were not in –
I saw so many forms that it almost made me grin;
Sally Ann was frying sausingers for Bob, the butcher's man,
So I asked the inclination of my charming Sally Ann.

33

5 O Sally in a passion flew saying: 'Boy, what do you mean?'
I said: 'My handsome Sally I'm not altogether green!'
She says: 'You made a promise and you're in this trap, young man –
So come leave my house, you savage!' cried my charming Sally Ann.

6 O I asked her for my jewelry that I had given her.
Quite angry she looked at me, like a wildcat she did purr;
When Sally in a passion flew and whipped the frying pan,
And she knocked me hipsy tipsy! She's my charming Sally Ann.

7 O I met a policeman on the road, my story I did tell –
I gave him a silver dollar and it seemed to please him well;
I took him back to Sally's house and o'er the place he ran –
But the devil a fragment could he find of charming Sally Ann.

8 O the old man he came home from work and my story I did tell,
That Sally Ann was runned away with Bob the butcher's man;
The old man he swore he'd have the life out of the butcher's man,
The old woman she swore vengeance on her daughter Sally Ann.

9 O the old man in a passion whipped his good ol' span of grey,
He whipped his horse and swore an oath in a good old-fashioned way;
And right ahead he spied them driving a splendid span –
'Twas very soon he overtook his daughter Sally Ann.

10 O the old man in a passion he drove in a foreign swathe,
And with a shot they all swung out, they went head over heels;
Their heads was in the ashes and their heels was in the sand,
And three somersaults we got of them before they reached the land.

11 O the policeman in the scrummage he got a broken thigh –
The old man with the cudgeler hooked out the butcher's eye;
'Twas Sally and her mother tore their hair from hand to hand,
But she couldn't hold a candle to her daughter Sally Ann.

12 We took them up as prisoners and marched them back to town,
Where I got my gold watch again and also fifty pound;
Where I got all my jewelry, wasn't I a smart young man?
So here's good-bye without a sigh to charming Sally Ann!

It is really entertaining to watch Mr Power sing this song. His performance is punctuated with grins, winks, and nods at the women present and much knee-slapping and gesticulating. His grandchildren love to request 'Sally Ann' and squeals of delight are sure to accompany his singing.

Chrissey's Dick

21 Chrissey's Dick

Linda Slade
St John's, 1976

Sprightly

O Chris-sey went up to Aunt Mar- garet's to get a loan of her dick. Says
Ma- ry Ann to Chris-to- pher: 'Be sure and do it quick!' Says
Ma- ry Ann to Chris-to- pher: 'Be sure now don't you stop, for
you got plen-ty of bait to-day and you got to bait your pots.'

2 Chrissey went up to Aunt Margaret's and brought the dick down home:
'O isn't he a lovely bird, he's got a lovely comb.
Go in the house John Chesley and get 'en a piece of bread –
O isn't he a lovely bird, he's got the cutest head.'

3 The hens and chicks and all of them were feeded for the night,
When Chris got up in the morning, the dick he wasn't in sight;
Chrissey he jumped out of bed and stepped on Mary Ann's toes –
Says Mary Ann to Christopher: 'I though I heard 'en crow!'

4 'It rained so very hard last night, why didn't you bar 'en in?
For going through the woods today, you'll get wet right through the skin.'
'Wet or dry,' says Mary Ann, 'the dick you'll have to find –
Go on up to Aunt Margaret's, don't stop to look behind.'

5 Chrissey went up to Aunt Margaret's, the dick he wasn't there,
He felt so faint and frightened that he fell down on a chair;
He started off for home again not feeling very stout,
He fell down in a mud-hole and the mud ran in his mouth.

6 Chrissey jumped out of his breeches and tumbled to the door.
Says Mary Ann to Christopher: 'The dick is gone for sure.
Put on your clothes,' says Mary Ann, 'and go and look for him,
For you'll get nothing to eat today unless you bring 'en in.'

7 He started off for Hay Cove, the dicky for to find,
But when he got about half ways over he heard 'en cry behind;
He looked around there he was not looking very warm[1] –
He took the dick all by the tail and tucked 'en under his arm.

8 Says Mary Ann to Christopher: 'I'm glad you got 'en back,
   For if we lost Aunt Margaret's dick, we'd have to pay a whack.
   I'm gonna get some hens meself and raise our little chicks,
   Then we won't have to bother Aunt Margaret for her dick!'

1 The vowel in warm is pronounced like the vowel in farm to rhyme with arm. This
   pronunciation of the vowel 'a' in some dialects of Newfoundland English is most
   typically found in words such as form, storm, and fork, where the vowel precedes an 'r.'

'Chrissey's Dick' was composed in Harbour Buffet, Placentia Bay, about Chrissey Dicks's
dick! Apparently Chrissey Dicks was quite often the brunt of jokes, being an odd sort of
fellow, though the jokes were generally in good humour. This song seems to have been
first performed on stage as a play in the community.

22 The Wreck of the *Christabel*

1 Come all you men of Bonavis',
   Come list to what I say,
   And I will tell you what occurred
   Upon the Sabbath Day.

2 It was on the seventh of June
   In eighteen eighty five,
   The wind came to the N.N. East
   And the sea began to rise.

3 A schooner called the *Christabel*
   And she was good as new,
   Was anchored in the harbour
   Where other vessels do.

4 With nine so good a seamen
   As ever drunk a glass,
   The captain, mate, and boatswain
   And six before the mast.

5 It was early Sunday morning
   This gale came on to blow;
   No pen I'm sure can well describe
   What they did undergo.

6 The vessel she began to roll
   And her anchors they did fail;
   The *Christabel* was driving
   All in that dreadful gale.

7 To the rocks and breakers right astern
   She drifted more and more;
   The captain thought he would be lost
   Upon that rugged shore.

8 They cut away the spars
To try and save their lives;
And every man was on their best
With hatchets and with knives.

9 But their anchors they got hold again
And kept her there once more;
For death must have been their portion
If they drifted on that shore.

10 All through a long and dreary night
Their anchors they did hold;
And don't you think those anchors
Was worth their weight in gold.

11 Young Dorothy jumped in the boat
To try what he could do;
A heavy sea did strike the boat
And broke the rope in two.

12 He drifted all along the shore
All in an open boat;
It is hard to tell how that poor man
Did keep so long afloat.

13 He wove his hands to his comrades
On board of the *Christabel*;
Where that poor fellow is lying now
It is hard for man to tell.

14 Dorothy was a smart young man
The crew did like him well;
The captain said he was as good
As ever furled a sail.

15 It was on Monday morning
The wind began to slack;
Two boats rowed out of the harbour
And took them from the wreck.

16 They were manned by hardy fishermen
Well used to our shore;
And they did do their very best
And what could they do more.

17 They took off those noble seamen
And rowed away again;
And soon was in the harbour
From off that stormy main.

18 When they rowed in the harbour
And drew quite near the shore;
There was a crowd of people waiting
One hundred souls or more.

19 And now the storm is over
   The sea is calm once more;
   The like I never wish to see
   Upon our ruggèd shore.

The *Christabel* was wrecked on the shores of Bonavista on June 1885. I found this song in an old diary at Bonavista and have copied the words here exactly as they were written.

23 Come and I Will Sing You

Jack Carroll
Stephenville, 1980

Come and I will sing you. What will you sing me?

I will sing you one- o. What will the one be?

One the one lives all a- lone for ev- er- more shall be so.

Ten the ten com- mand- ments   nine the bright-eyed shin- ers

eight the Gab- riel an- gels   seven the seven stars un-der the sky

six the six bol wag- ers   five the flem boys un-der the bush

four the gos- pel crea- tures   three of them were driv- ers

two of them were li-ly white babes   clo-thèd all in green- o

one the one lives all a- lone   (for)ev- er more shall be so.

2 Come and I will sing you
What will you sing me?
I will sing you two-o
What will the two be?
Two of them were lily-white babes
Clothèd all in green-o
One the one lives all alone
Forever more shall be so.

[Continue adding lines up to ten]

10 Ten the Ten Commandments
Nine the bright-eyed shiners
Eight the Gabriel angels
Seven the seven stars under the sky
Six the six bol (bold/bowl?) wagers
Five the flem boys under the bush
Four the gospel creatures
Three of them were drivers
Two of them were lily-white babes
Clothèd all in green-o
One the one lives all alone
Forever more shall be so.

Originally from Red Island in Placentia Bay, Mr Carroll would step-dance while singing this song; his wife, Ellen, usually answered on the second and fourth line of each verse, acting as the second voice. Mr Carroll did not know the meaning of the song but felt that it was 'stuff from way back, really old, long before anybody's time.' And, indeed, this religious song seems to be of some antiquity, having both Christian and Hebrew versions.

Known also as the Ten Commandments and the Twelve Apostles, this cumulative song has enjoyed much popularity among folksingers in the southwest of England and throughout North America. Though it has been extensively collected, it is still a curiosity and somewhat of a puzzle to folksong scholars. For an interesting discussion on the subject, see *One Hundred English Folk Songs*, edited by Cecil Sharp (New York: Dover Publications, Inc. 1975).

MERCER 189

24 Common Sailors

Moses Harris
Lethbridge, 1976

I'm the man be-fore the mast, that ploughs the rag-ing sea and on this sim-ple sub-ject will you please en-light-en me: Com-mon sail-ors we are called, come tell me the rea-son why and on this sim-ple sub-ject I'll re-ply;

[Chorus:]

don't you call us com-mon sail-ors an-y more; don't you call us com-mon sail-ors an-y more; good things to you we bring, don't you call us com-mon men, we're as good as an-y-bo-dy that's on shore.

2 The young girls of this country, their growing days we bless
We brings them silks and satins out of which they makes a dress;
To gain the heart of some young man as fancy dresses do –
Don't never despise the sailor boys that sails the ocean blue.

Chorus:

Don't you call us common sailors any more,
Don't you call us common sailors any more;
Good things to you we bring, don't you call us common men,
We're as good as anybody that's on shore.

3 The young gents of this country, they're sitting at their ease
　Not thinking on the stormy nights that we spent on the seas;
　We brings the leaves to make cigars to decorate their face –
　They wouldn't call us common if they were sometimes in our place.

As far as I know, 'Common Sailors' has appeared in print only once before, in the book
Manavilins by Rex Clements. The author describes his collection as 'A muster of sea-songs,
as distinguished from shanties, written for the most part by seamen, and sung on board
Ship during the closing years of the Age of Sail, 1890-1910.' Mr Clements writes that
'Common Sailors' is 'A ballad of a different calibre and unusual altogether . . . It possessed
an interminable number of verses, and was often heard at sea in the early days of the
present century.' He goes on to say that the song 'was popular among Colonial seamen'
and that his version 'may represent an Australian version of the original.' Verse 2 of Mr
Clements runs:

When speaking of a man ashore we never hear you say
He's a 'common' this or 'common' that, be his calling what it may;
Be he a travelling tinker, or a scavenger, or sweep,
Then why call us 'common' sailors who battle with the deep?

This song would undoubtedly have been a boost to the morale of many's the sea-faring
man who was so often derided by disdainful land-dwellers.

25 Constant Farmer's Son

Johnny Tobias Pearson
Southeast Bight, 1979

Slowly, with a gentle lilt

'Tis of a comely mai- den living by a riv- er
-side, she was both tall and beau- ti- ful, they
called her the vil-lage pride. Rich lords came to court
her but their love was all in vain for there was
one, a farm-er's son, young Ma- ry's heart did gain.

42

2 They pledged their love together and planned their wedding day.
  Her mother and father gave their consent, but her brothers this did say:
  'There is a squire now courting you, and him you must not shun,
  Or else, this day we will betray your constant farmer's son.'

3 Those brothers they got ready and then they went straightway
  To seek young Willy's company, for to spend with him one day;
  But on the way returning home his glass of life was run –
  'Twas with a knife they took the life of her constant farmer's son.

4 Young Mary on her pillow lay, that night could get no rest
  With thoughts of her own Willy burning deep within her breast.
  Mary arose, put on her clothes and to seek her love did run,
  It was dead and cold she did behold her constant farmer's son.

5 It was dead and cold she did behold him bleeding in yon grove.
  The tears ran down her lovely face, she kissed him o'er and o'er.
  She plucked the green leaves from the trees for to shade him from the sun;
  It was night and day she pined away for her constant farmer's son.

6 'Til hunger came approaching this fair one all alone,
  To seek her brothers' company she quickly went home.
  Saying: 'Brothers dear, you soon shall hear of the cruel deed you've done –
  You have done the deed and now must bleed like my constant farmer's son.'

7 Up speaks the eldest brother: 'I'm sure it was not me!'
  Up speaks the youngest brother who swore most bitterly;
  'Oh brothers dear, you need not swear for the cruel deed you've done,
  You'll rue the day that you did slay my constant farmer's son!'

8 Those brothers they were taken and very soon were tried,
  Young Mary on her pillow lay, she never ceased to cry.
  Those brothers they decayed away, for their glass of life was run.
  Young Mary sighed and in sorrow died for her constant farmer's son.

This is a song I learned from Tobias Pearson of Merasheen. It is a version of a very old song known variously as 'The Pot of Basil,' 'Bruton Town,' and 'The Cruel Brothers.' A.B.

26 The Wreck of the *Danny Goodwin*

Jerry Fudge
McCallum, 1977

Come all you peo- ple far and near, come lis- ten to my song, in lan- guage I'll ex- -plain to you, it won't de- lay you long; come hear a- bout Cap-tain La- Fosse who late- ly took com- mand, in the schoo- ner called the Dan- ny from New Har- bour, New- found- land.

2 Sailing away from New Harbour, to the western shores did go,
To risk their lives in dories, through frost and wind and snow;
Saying good-bye to friends at home, and all whom they adore,
Never dreaming that they'd meet their doom upon the western shore.

3 It was on a Monday morning they got her underway,
The sixth day of December, a fine, cold winter's day;
She carried a crew of six fishermen, and dories she had two,
And the *Danny* being a noble boat, all builded over new.

4 On Rose Blanche banks that morning, 'twas there he brought her to,
He lowered away his dories as he oft-times used to do;
Before those trawls were taken back a heavy sea did rise,
It was a hard and a trying time for those poor sailor boys.

5 The wind veered from the east-south-east and bitterly did blow;
The sea was rolling mountains high, a blinding drift of snow.
No doubt he may have come to land, all under close-reef sails,
Or perhaps he got disabled in the terrible winter's gale.

6 A captain from another boat, those words we heard him say:
'He did not have his dories when we got underway.
He may not have had his dories we do not understand,
Perhaps he got them safe on board and shaped her for the land.'

7 To come to land that evening through blinding sleet and snow,
Our captain being a stranger and those harbours did not know;
No doubt he may have come to land or he may have run ashore,
Perhaps he drifted far out to sea to never return no more.

8 There's five poor widows left behind who bitterly will cry,
All thinking of their loved ones who in the deep do lie;
Their wives and little children they'll never see no more,
Who now gave up all hopes to die upon the western shore.

9 The blow was hard for friends at home, the sad news for to tell,
The loss of sons and husbands, the ones they loved so dear;
Likewise their agèd mothers who bitterly will cry;
Saying: 'There's some leaving their homes wishing them all good-bye.'

10 So now my song is ended I have nothing more to say.
Trying to earn a living those boys were called away.
Their wives and their little children they'll never see no more,
Who now gave up all hopes to die upon the western shore.

New Harbour is presumably the New Harbour on the Southwest Coast, a particularly
dangerous and treacherous area of the coastline where countless ships have been wrecked
and lost without a trace.

MERCER 149

27 The Dark-eyed Sailor

Kate Wilson
Placentia, 1977

It's a-bout a mai-den was young and fair, walked out one eve-ning to take the air; she met a sai-lor all on the way, and she paid at-ten-tion, and she paid at-ten-tion to hear what he did say.

2 Said Willie: 'Maiden, why roam alone?
The night is coming and the day far gone.'
She said while tears from her eyes did flow:
'It's my dark-eyed sailor –
It's my dark-eyed sailor is the cause of all my woe.

3 It's six long years since he left this land,
A gold ring he took from off my hand;
Broke it in two, left a part with me,
Whilst the other lies rolling –
Whilst the other lies rolling in the bottom of the sea.'

4 Said Willie: 'Drive him far from your mind,
A better sailor than him you'll find;
Love turns aside and cold do grow,
Like a winter's morning –
Like a winter's morning when the hills are clad with snow.'

5 O this did her fond heart enflame.
She said; 'On me you won't play no game;
A man he was, not a rat like you
To advise a maiden –
To advise a maiden to slight her jacket blue.

6 His tarry trousers I'll never disdain,
But I will always treat him the same;
To drink his health, here's a piece of coin
For that dark-eyed sailor –
For that dark-eyed sailor still claims the heart of mine.'

7 Then half the ring did young Willie show,
   She fell distracted amidst grief and woe.
   'You're welcome Willie, I have land and gold
   For my dark-eyed sailor –
   For my dark-eyed sailor so manly, true, and bold.'

8 Now in a cottage down by the sea,
   They're joined in wedlock and do agree.
   So maids be true whilst your love's away,
   For a cloudy morning –
   For a cloudy morning brings forth a pleasant day!

This is one of the most popular of the numerous broken-ring ballads. It is most perplexing
that the sailor could pull such a hoax on the fair maid. Mrs Kate once remarked that if she
had been the lady in question, he would have had to 'hike off' for another six years.

MERCER 112

28 Dark-eyed Susan

Elsie Best
St John's, 1977

Gently

All in the downs where the fleet lay moored with
stream-ers wav-ing in the wind, when dark-eyed Su-san came on
board, saying: "Where will I my true love
find? Tell me ye jo-vial sai-lors, tell
me, o tell me true if my love Will-iam, if my love
Wil-liam sails a-mong your crew."

2 William was high up in the yard,
   Tossed by the billows to and fro;
   Soon as her well-known voice he heard,
   He sighed and cast his eyes below.
   The cord slides swiftly through his glowing hands
   And quick as lightning,
   And quick as lightning, on the deck he stands.

3 So the sweet lark high-poised in the air,
   Shuts close his pinions to his breast;
   If chance his mate's shrill call he hears,
   And drops at once into her nest.
   The noblest captain in the British fleet
   Might envy William,
   Might envy William's lips those kisses sweet.

4 'O Susan, Susan, o lovely dear,
   My vows shall ever true remain;
   Let me kiss off that falling tear –
   We only part to meet again.
   Change as ye list, ye winds, my heart shall be
   The faithful compass,
   The faithful compass that still points to thee.

5 Believe not what the landsmen say,
   Who tempt with doubts thy constant mind;
   They'll tell thee sailors when away
   In every port a sweetheart find.
   Yes, yes, believe them when they tell thee so
   For thou art present,
   For thou art present wheresoe'er I go.

6 If to fair India's coast we sail,
   Thine eyes are seen in diamonds bright;
   Thy breath in Africa's spicy gale –
   Thy skin is ivory so white.
   Thus every beauteous object that I view
   Wakes in my soul,
   Wakes in my soul some charms of lovely Sue.

7 Though battle calls me from thine arms,
   Let not my pretty Susan mourn;
   Though cannons roar, yet safe from harm
   William shall to his dear return.
   Love turns aside the balls that 'round me fly
   Lest precious tears,
   Lest precious tears should drop from Susan's eyes.'

8 The bosun gave the dreadful word,
   The sails their swelling bosoms spread;
   No longer must she stay on board –
   They kissed, she sighed, he hung his head.
   Her listing boat unwilling sped to land
   'Adieu,' she cried,
   'Adieu,' she cried, and waved her lily hand.

My mother brought this song with her from Tack's Beach when she moved to Merasheen, Placentia Bay. Lillian Pittman learned it from her and wrote it down in her song scribbler. The scribbler was lost in the move to Placentia during the Resettlement era, but the song survived. Great was my surprise to find out, much later, that John Gay of Beggar's Opera fame had composed it in 1760, and that our version matched his almost word for word. A.B.

29 The Steamship *Deane*

Mary (Min) Caul
Arnold's Cove, 1976

You peo-ple all both great and small I hope you will at-tend and lis-ten to those ver-ses few that I have late-ly penned, while I re-late the hard-ships great that fish-er-men must stand while sail-ing o-ver the stor-my seas on the coast of New-found-land.

2 It happened to be in the summertime in the lovely month of June
The flowers began to spring and rise all in their earthly bloom;
If you will pay attention I will unfold to ye
The dangers of the S.S. *Deane* that went out on the sea.

3 She left the port of Harbour Grace being on a Sunday night
With a crew of hearty whaling men with spirits gay and bright;
For to land them in Hawke's Harbour as she oft-times done before
But now I'm sorry to relate she'll never go no more.

49

4 She left the port of Harbour Grace when flowers were in full bloom
  To land them in Hawke's Harbour her summer to pursue;
  With fifty brave whaling men of courage brave and gay
  The most of them were married men, belong to Placentia Bay.

5 She left the port of Harbour Grace as we have all been told
  Not fearing any danger no matter how it blowed;
  And on that very same Sunday to our surprising shock
  The S.S. *Deane* making full speed she lands upon a rock.

6 And when she struck upon the rock 'twas a sad sight for to see
  Every man with his clothes bag as witty as could be;
  For to save their belongings that was money's worth to them
  And struggling hard to save their lives those fifty shipwrecked men.

7 You may thank the light keeper that lived on Penguin,
  The lovely man, whoever he was, all praise be given him;
  May this good deed go down for him, may it recorded be
  For saving those fifty shipwrecked men from the dangers of the sea.

8 For to conclude and finish, thank God no deed was done
  The *Deane* she sank to rise no more so near Stag Harbour run;
  They're safely in Hawke's Harbour their summer for to spend
  May God be with them night and day, send them safe home again.

The *Deane* was wrecked 23 June 1935 on the North Penguin Shoals, near Musgrave Harbour. She was owned by the Newfoundland Whaling Company and commanded by Captain Bronneck.

30 The Dole Song

John (Jack) Lushman, Sr
Ramea, 1977

You asked me to sing you a song, I'll do the
best I can, for when a man goes
on the dole his troubles are just be-gun.
It is the case of an-y man in eve-ry
port a-round; you first give in your
state-ment, and then they'll write it down.

2 First they'll ask you what's your name, and then ask what you've got;
  A few old raggedy lines of gear and a few old lobster pots.
  To see what trouble a man has got and he has to tell them so;
  Be careful boys, don't tell no lies when you goes on the dole.

3 Now the winter is over and spring will soon be here;
  You'll see them with their fires all in, all tanning up their gear.
  All painting up their motor-boats and dories too, likewise;
  They're at it in the morning before the sun do rise.

4 Now it's time for fishing we will try to get some bait;
  Hurry up and put a rush on boys, before it is too late.
  For the man who got the motor-boat he haven't got to row;
  He has to work both day and night to keep away from dole.

5 Now the fishing is over the next is the caplin scull;
  From Fortune to Grand Bank my boys, and from that to Dantzic Cove
  We'll take on board our caplin boys, and we'll then bait up our gear;
  We'll stick her to the Western Grounds if the weather it do keep clear.

6 Now it's time to haul it back, the fish is very scarce;
   The wind veered down about west-north-west and blowing very fierce.
   We only got two tubs that day, the rest we could not get;
   A man he must be crazy boys, to come up here and sit.

7 Tommy Garland he's our merchant and that you all do know.
   He turned off some of his planters and they had to go on the dole;
   After working all the summer you could cut it all the year,
   And in the fall go on the dole, we do not call it square.

8 The man who got the money boys, you know he is all right;
   He got the best to eat and drink, tobacco in his pipe.
   But a day will come for him to die and be put down in the hole,
   And then he'll have no better chance than the poor man on the dole.

Mr Lushman informed me that Tommy Garland was a merchant in Gaultois on the
Southwest Coast. The composer of the song, he said, was also from there, though he did
not know the person's name when the song was written.
   The indignity of having to go on the dole was endured by many a Newfoundland
fisherman when fishing was exceptionally poor. Of course, the local merchant (as the song
suggests) was often only interested in his own profit and had scant concern for the plight
of the fishermen who depended on him for supplies to last the winter, and even sometimes
for work.

31 The Drunken Captain

Pius Power, Jr
Southeast Bight, 1983

In St. John's ci-ty our ves-sel lay
when our drun-ken cap-tain went on a spree; he
came on board and to us did say: "Get your
le-vers rea-dy, b'ys, and heave a-way."

2 We got her ready by his command,
The wind blew free as we left the land –
We left Cape Pine all on our lee
And we sprang her out in the deep blue sea.

3 Down came a squall from the angry sky,
She pitched and plunged but she wouldn't lie.
Our jib and jibbets came to the wind;
We took in our jib and new sheets did bend.

4 Our mate came up with the devil's fright
Sayin': 'B'ys she's filling through the big skylight.'
Sayin': 'Captain if you don't shorten sail
We'll all be lost in this heavy gale.'

5 Our captain swore on the deck that day
He'd shoot the first man to touch a sail.
He cursed and swore: 'If the winds do blow
I'll show you all how my ship can go.'

6 Then up speaks one of our gallant band:
'Here's twelve of us on this deck do stand;
We'll reef her down, to the seas we'll go,
If you interfere you'll be tied below.'

So we reefed her down but against his will –
The wind blew steady and her sails did fill;
We're heading home along the Cape Shore now
As she spreads the white foam out from her bow.

8 Now we're bound home with joy and success
Like a lonely sea-gull she seeks her nest.
When I gets on shore nevermore I'll sail
With a drunken captain in a heavy gale
When I gets on shore nevermore I'll sail
With you George Mattas in the *Florabelle*!

This song is also known in Nova Scotia as 'Canso Strait' with the following first verse:

In Canso Strait our vessel lay,
We just arrived in from the bay,
Our vessel built both stout and strong
To Gloucester she does belong.

It would appear to have been composed in Newfoundland, but could very well have been written in Nova Scotia.

MERCER 114

53

The *Ella M. Rudolph*

32 The *Ella M. Rudolph*

Moses Harris
Lethbridge, 1976

At-ten-tion all ye fish-er-men and toil-ers of the sea while I re-late those lines to you of an aw-ful tra-ge-dy, which leaves so ma-ny fa-mi-lies in sor-row to be-wail the loss of sons and hus-bands caused by the dread-ful gale.

2 The *Ella M. Rudolph* a vessel, and such a clever sea boat too
   Her skipper's name was Blackwood, and eight composed her crew;
   A female also was on board, so gaily and bright –
   She with the rest did meet her doom on that sad fatal night.

3 The sixth day of December the *Rudolph* leaved the town
   Full loaded with general cargo for Port Nelson she was bound;
   With a gentle breeze of southwest winds the schooner sailed along
   The sky looked thick and heavy and night was coming on.

4 At five o'clock in the evening through the Tickles she did pass
   The threatening of a violent storm was showing by the glass;
   When from south-east the wind did veer and storms all through the night –
   It was our skipper's intention to make Catalina light.

5 Not very far out in the bay the schooner did she reach
   When the skipper changed his course again from north unto north-east;
   Thinking the ship would round the Cape, reach Bonavista Bay
   'Twas under her foresail and jumbo she unfortunately made leeway.

6 Eight fine strong men that very night upon her deck did stand
  With piercing eyes and eager hearts all on the look-out for land;
  The wind blowed strong, the seas rose high, o what a terrible plight!
  The *Ella M. Rudolph* ended her days on Catalina shores that night.

7 The vessel scarcely struck a rock 'fore covered with the waves –
  All of her crew except one man did meet a watery grave;
  This poor young chap jumped overboard through blinding snow and drift
  By the guiding hands of Providence was hurled into the cliff.

8 He wended his way on up the cliff through blinding sleet and snow –
  Over marshes, fields, and valleys not knowing where to go
  To look for hospitality and comfort for the night;
  When to his surprise before his eyes saw Little Catalina light.

9 'Twas early the next morning about the hour of four
  After eight long hours of travelling, reached Levi Dalton's door;
  Who kindly answered to his knock, such a sadful sight to see –
  A lad stood there with oilclothes on, a miracle for him to see.

10 'Come in my lad, come in my lad,' this kind man he did say,
  'And tell us what has happened and how you came this way.'
  The lad was so exhausted, and all that he could say,
  'A schooner lost and all her crew not very far away.'

11 Now with this kindly woman this poor lad did reside
  After hot drinks and clothing warm she soon did him revive;
  And after rest and medical aid, the tale he told anew –
  The sorrowful fate of the *Rudolph* and the loss of all her crew.

12 This man soon told his neighbours and soon the news was spread
  And men before 'twas very long was rising from their beds;
  With gaffs and ropes and lanterns on a night so dark and drear
  The path was thronged with men and for Brook Cove they did steer.

13 At last they arrived upon the spot but sadly heard no sound –
  They searched in vain with daring but no creatures could be found;
  When a sadful sight came before their eyes as they stood there next day
  To see a body wash ashore all on a heaving wave.

14 This chanced to be the female, one so gaily with fame –
  An Abbott girl from Hare Bay, her name was Mary Jane;
  And soon with kind and willing hands her body did prepare
  And sent along for her burial rites to her mother's home so dear.

15 But two more bodies still are lying beneath the ocean waves
  Waiting for the Saviour's call on the last great Judgment Day;
  When the sea it will give up its dead we're told by scripture true –
  May the Lord have mercy on the souls of the *Ella M. Rudolph*'s crew.

According to Mr G.J. Casey, who collected a version of the *Ella M. Rudolph* in Cape Broyle, the song was written by Hugh Sexton and Dukey Blackwood, and appeared in the *Trinitarian*, Trinity, Newfoundland, on 21 December 1926. Mr Gordon S.A. Cox also collected a version of the song in Trinity Bay and notes that several of his informants knew Dukey Blackwood, the lone survivor of the *Rudolph* and co-author of the song.

Uncle Mose Harris said this song was printed on broadsheets and sold around Bonavista Bay to raise money for the families of those lost aboard the vessel.

33 The *Elsie M. Hart*

Benedict Keough
Plate Cove, 1976

Come all ye hear-ty sea-men, come lis-ten to my song, it
is both short and sim-ple it will not de-lay you long; con-
cer-ning of a schoo-ner that sailed from Tri-ni-ty Bay, on the
eigh-teenth of No-vem-ber, I think it was the day.

2 Her name it was the *Elsie M. Hart*, Captain March was in command.
Steven Pelley from Random Island on her was second hand.
Her crew was composed of four men more, their names I will not say.
She had on board some merchandise for a port down in White Bay.

3 The day being dull and cloudy and dismal looked the sky,
And coming on towards evening the wind began to rise;
As they were off Bonavista Cape, that place called Happy Sight,
The skipper said he would heave to, and rest up for the night.

4 The snow came down in torrents, proud Boreas did advance;
When the sleet and snow from the east did blow to the windward you could
    not glance.
The sea did run mountainously and the vessel she made leeway,
In spite of with her foresail split, she had to run the bay.

5 They sat their course for Plate Cove as near as they could go,
'Twas under the skirt of her mainsail and part of her jumbo;
As she ran o'er the Western Shores they thought they were no more,
At two o'clock next morning the vessel ran on shore.

6 Just imagine these poor seamen upon an unknown strand,
It being so dark and stormy they did not know the land.
At daybreak there that morning, to their surprise and joy,
They saw by their surroundings, some livyers they were nigh.

7 The captain and another man got landed safe on shore,
At that place called Hurra Point [sic] where the angry billows roar;
Up hills and through the forest with difficulty roamed,
And early there that morning they broke out at Plate Cove.

57

8 They related their sad story and they received a helping hand.
  People rushed onto the shores to assist the other men.
  And now they're landed safe on shore, I know they won't complain,
  May the Lord assist those seamen that ploughs the raging main.

This shipwreck took place on 18 November 1935, close to the community of Plate Cove, Bonavista Bay. The *Elsie M. Hart* was en route to Port aux Choix from Trinity Bay with a load of freight when she ran ashore. The crew were hospitably treated by the people of Plate Cove, and Mr Mike Keough of that community composed this song about the event. I recorded the song from his son, Mr Benedict Keough, at Plate Cove.

34 The *Excel* (A)

Mary (Min) Caul
Arnold's Cove, 1977

Slowly, with feeling

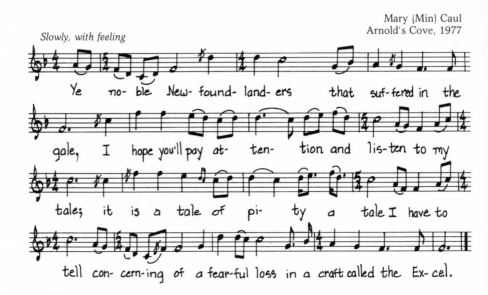

Ye no-ble New-found-land-ers that suf-fered in the
gale, I hope you'll pay at-ten-tion and lis-ten to my
tale; it is a tale of pi-ty a tale I have to
tell con-cern-ing of a fear-ful loss in a craft called the Ex-cel.

2 On the eighth day of October when everything was gay,
  We hoisted our flag up to the mast all for to go away;
  Before that we were ready a gale came on to blow,
  And with it hove a heavy swell and also showers of snow.

3 We quickly then got ready our vessel to secure,
  We worked away all that long day 'til we could do no more;
  To watch our lines and keep them served the night until 'twas day –
  'Twould be better if our lines had parted, we might have run to sea.

4 We trusted to God's mercy, who always answered prayer,
  He showed us the way to save ourselves, likewise our little gear;
  'Twas true we did not follow Him, but trusted our own to fate –
  And left us here cold mourners, our sorrow to relate.

5 We worked all that long summer, and hard both day and night,
  To earn bread for our children and that with all our might;
  Now some of them are sleeping beneath the briny wave –
  Some more of them are buried down in Black Island graves.

6 Being on a Sunday morning when the wind did roar and rage,
  There was twenty-two of the *Excel* crew met with a watery grave;
  There was men, women, and children stood on her quarter-deck,
  When a heavy sea broke over her and swept them from the wreck.

7 There was one man in our number, his locks were turning grey,
  He stood apart from all the rest his thoughts so far away;
  On the rugged shore of the Labrador where this cruel deed was done,
  In a place called the Black Island, outside of Grady's Run.

The *Excel* (B)

Dorman Ralph
St John's, 1977

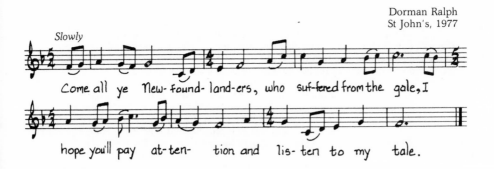

Come all ye Newfoundlanders, who suffered from the gale, I
hope you'll pay attention and listen to my tale.

2 It is a tale of pity, that which I have to tell
  Concerning of that fatal wreck in a vessel called the *Excel*.

3 On the rocky shore on the Labrador, where the dreadful deed was done
  In a place called the Black Island, outside of Grady's Run.

4 Where we had spent our summer in working day and night
  To earn bread for our family, and that with all our might.

5 On the tenth day of October the wind began to blow
  And that with it a heavy sea, and likewise showers of snow.

6 We then prepared, got ready, when everything looked grey;
  We hoisted our colours to the mast, hoping to sail next day.

7 We then prepared, got ready, our vessel to secure
  And after everything was done, we could do nothing more.

8 Only watch our lines and keep secured, praying to God for help
  Thinking if our vessel should be lost, we all hands might be saved.

9 We prayed to the Almighty One, the One who answers prayer,
  Thinking that our vessel might be lost, likewise our little gear.

10 But He would not hearken or obey, we trusted alone in faith;
    It leaves me here a mourner, my story to relate.

11 The women and the children, stood on her quarter-deck
    When a heavy sea flowed over her, and swept them from the wreck.

12 Among this fateful number, there was one whose locks were grey,
    He stood apart so moderate, his mind seemed far away.

13 When all was calm and silent, those screeching could be heard
    For they was hurled in instantly, to the prison of their Lord.

14 This dreadful night is passed and gone, its marks are left behind
    It is a warning for ye all, to prepare while it is time.

15 To meet your friends and loved ones, the ones whom you adore
    On the blissful shores of Canaan, where partings are no more.

The following story, entitled 'Out of the Past – The Great Tragedy – 1885,' is from *The Daily News*, 28 March 1957:

'The greatest sea tragedy involving people of Coley's Point was the loss of the schooner *Excel* at Black Island, near Grady, on Oct. 11, 1885, with a loss of about twenty-two men, women and children. Three or four bodies that were recovered were brought home for burial; others were buried at Black Island. Some were not recovered.

'The *Excel* was in charge of Capt. George Morgan, father of Mr. John Morgan, and was anchored outside Black Island waiting suitable time to sail for home. A gale came on Saturday night, continuing through Sunday. At 12 o'clock Sunday night, the ship parted her chains and was driven ashore. Heavy seas began to sweep over the decks and so the Captain ordered the spars to be cut away. The foremast, in falling, broke into three pieces, the top of the mainmast lodged for awhile on the shore. Miss Emma Jane Roach (afterwards Mrs. W.H. Littlejohn), the only female survivor, with others, sought refuge from the seas by standing in the hatchway. She seized the opportunity to escape by quickly jumping on the spar and using it as a bridge to reach the land. There she clung to the rocks and kelp in the raging sea until she was dragged to safety by Mr. Stephen Russell who was on the shore. This brave woman had just reached the shore when the spar broke, carrying away with it two men, William Batten and Abram Morgan who were attempting the same means of escape. The Capt. and several members of his family were lost. A complete list of those lost is not available as several were passengers (freighters) from other places.'

35 False Limkin

Moses Harris
Lethbridge, 1976

Ominously

Said the lord to his la-dy: "I am go-ing a-way, be-ware of false Lim-kin he don't lead you a-stray. I don't care for Lim-kin or no o-ther man, for my doors are fast bol-ted and he can-not get in."

2 Limkin came there 'bout the middle of the night,
   He called on his jewel his own heart's delight;
   'O where is your mistress,' false Limkin did say –
   'She is in the top tower,' said the false nurse to he.

3 Said proud Limkin to the false nurse: 'How will I get her down?'
   Said the false nurse to the Limkin: 'Hit the babe on the crown.
   I can't quiet your baby with breast-milk or pap,
   So I pray you fair lady come and daddle it on your lap.'

4 'How can I come down on a cold winter's night,
   With no fire burning nor no candle light?'
   'You have got three candles so bright as the sun,
   So I pray you fair lady come down by the light of one.'

5 As the lady was coming down not thinking no harm
   The Limkin betrayed her, caught her by the arm;
   'I've got you! I've got you!' false Limkin did cry –
   'And it's more to my sorrow,' that poor lady replied.

6 'Come here daughter Betsy, those few words I will speak
   And hold a silver basin, your heart's blood I'll take;'
   O no, daughter Betsy, I pray stay alone
   And try for to see your dear father come home.'

7 As Betsy was gazing through the window so high,
   She saw her dear father a-riding close by;
   Saying 'Father, dear father, I pray don't blame me –
   'Twas the false nurse and the Limkin betrayed your lady.'

8 There was blood in the kitchen, there was blood in the hall –
  There was blood in the cradle, it was worse than all;
  The Limkin was hung on the gallows so high
  And the false nurse was burned on the mountain near by.

One night while staying at Uncle Mose's, I asked him if he had ever heard the old song
'Bold Lamkin,' and I described the story to him. He replied that it was very interesting but
he had never heard it before. Very early next morning, I was astonished to hear him sing
the whole song as he was lighting the fire in the kitchen. He told me he had completely
forgotten that he had known it.

  According to William Motherwell in *Minstrelsy: Ancient and Modern*, Limkin is actually
Lambert Linkin, the revengeful builder of Prime Castle – for which work he was not paid
by the lord. 'Antiquaries,' says Motherwell, 'peradventure, may find it as difficult to settle
the precise locality of this fortalice, as they have found it to fix the topography of Troy.'

MERCER 143

36 Fanny's Harbour Bawn

Pius Power, Sr
Southeast Bight, 1980

Free time

As I roamed out one eve-ning in the love-ly month of May, those ver-dant hills I ram-bled to view the dis-tant bay; the craft were flock-ing down the shore and plea-sant looked the day, when to my sur-prise a pair I spied that caused me to de-lay.

2 'Twas there I saw a young man embracing fondly,
  The charms of a fair one that once was loved by me;
  My heart with jealous notions felt eagerly the wrong,
  Which caused this fearful contest on Fanny's Harbour Bawn.

3 I did address this young man and unto him did say,
  'Are you from Bonavista or are you from the Bay?
  I think you are a northernman, a bay man I presume;
  So I pray be gone all from this bawn or I'll boot you in your bloom.

62

4 He quickly made an answer, and this to me did say:
   'I'm not from Bonavista, but I am from that Bay;
   I do reside where storms and tide have swept down buildings strong,
   Here in full glee from T. and C. to meet you on the Bawn.'

5 I stood no hesitation, but struck immediately.
   This damsel mild stood like a child to witness the fray;
   A pain then in my chest he rose before 'twas very long,
   My person pucked and my darking 'tuk' on Fanny's Harbour Bawn.

6 He skinned my nose from my face as I instantly did rise,
   And soon unto my regal brow he joined a bunch of fives;
   Which left me there prostrated, quite lifeless on the Bawn,
   And when I came to my senses the bay man he was gone.

7 Now when you meet with a northernman you'll think he's somewhat green,
   You'll treat him with a scornful look as unfit to be seen;
   You'll scoff them and rebuke them all with a scolding tongue,
   'Til you enrage, in a fight engage, from a bay man you will run.

8 I will not fail to tell the tale nor yet my true love's name;
   Her name is Catherine Murphy, she dwells in Roger's Lane.
   And I'm a youth from Carbonear once loved by her I know,
   My curse attend that northernman that proved by overthrow.

9 Now to conclude those painful lines, from courting I'll refrain,
   And likewise my companions I hope they'll do the same.
   For in courting there's great jealousy, and likewise envy strong,
   Which caused my claret blood to flow on Fanny's Harbour Bawn.

This song was written by Mark Walker of Tickle Cove (T. and C.), Bonavista Bay. The incident described in the song apparently took place in the mid-1800s – the young damsel being a native of St John's.

MERCER 118

37 Fishing on the Labrador

Moses Harris
Lethbridge, 1976

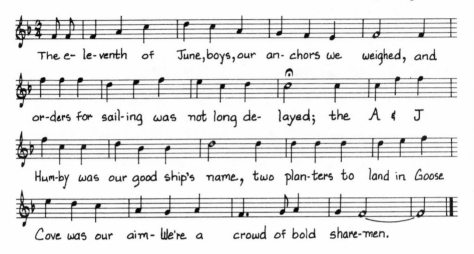

The e-le-venth of June, boys, our an-chors we weighed, and or-ders for sail-ing was not long de-layed; the A & J Hum-by was our good ship's name, two plan-ters to land in Goose Cove was our aim- We're a crowd of bold share-men.

2 We arrived there at Goose Cove 'twas early at dawn,
We landed our planters and then we went on;
We hoisted up our foresail to the fair wind and tide,
And away for St Anthony our good ship did slide
We're a crowd of hold sharemen.

3 We leaved the next morning the weather being fair;
Got out in the straits and bold Neptune appeared.
Two men took a shave, you all know them well;
To bring it in rhyme 'tis Burt Downey and Bill
We're a crowd of bold sharemen.

4 We got to Indian Tickles ...
    . . .

We went up the bay some ducks we knocked down,
And on the way back a man nearly got drowned
We're a crowd of bold sharemen.

5 His name is Burt Downey he's not very old,
He stood on the seat, the tiller controlled;
Coming up to our vessel the tiller slipped out,
And out in the water he sloused all about
We're a crowd of bold sharemen.

6 We leaved the next morning the weather being fair;
Got out in Groswater we meet the ice there.
We lowered down our canvas and steamed all around,
And into Sloop Harbour our anchor went down
We're a crowd of bold sharemen.

7 We leaved the next morning the weather being fine,
   The berths at Cape Harrison was strong in our minds;
   But when we got there the ice hove us back,
   Went up to Jigger Tickles the ice it was slack
   We're a crowd of bold sharemen.

8 We got to Jigger Tickles and there moored her up;
   Took a berth to Cape Dale and the two Golden Cups.
   We went up the bay to cut some dry wood,
   We killed five young seals, and I think we done good
   We're a crowd of bold sharemen.

9 We fished there a month boys, what could we do more.
   We hoisted in our boats for to go down the shore;
   Expecting good news but what did we find,
   A main jam of ice and fish only a sign
   We're a crowd of bold sharemen.

10 We went to the Savages the sky looking black;
   Our skipper said: 'Now boys, we'll put out a trap.'
   The glass going down, but still we pressed on,
   Went out in the morning and everything gone
   We're a crowd of bold sharemen.

11 The summer is ended and we are so proud
   I'll try if I can to name out her crowd;
   There's Henry and Horace in the white punt it's true,
   Uncle Dick and Pat Ayles in the one painted blue
   We're a crowd of bold sharemen.

12 Jim Humby is captain, Bill Lane second hand.
   Mose Harris is cook and he don't give a damn.
   Harv Elliot and George you all know them well,
   Two more I will mention, Burt Downey and Bill
   We're a crowd of bold sharemen.

13 Next comes is John, he's nice and he's fair
   Then it is Rex, our chief engineer;
   He is a fine fellow, I said nothing wrong,
   He sets going the engine that drives her along
   We're a crowd of bold sharemen.

14 Now to conclude those few lines I have wrote,
   To make a fair voyage we all had to scote;
   To make up our wages we all were inclined,
   Four boats and three codtraps, our jiggers and lines
   We're a crowd of bold sharemen.

'Fishing on the Labrador' is one of Uncle Mose's compositions. It was written while he
was at the Savage Islands on the Labrador coast. During that summer, he was cook on the
vessel *A & J Humby* from Summerville, Bonavista Bay.

38 The *Florizel*

Elsie Best
St John's, 1983

At- ten- tion fel- low coun-try- men while this sad tale I'll tell, a- bout the well-known steam- ship, the S. S. Flo- ri- zel; when grave- ly harmed up near Re- news the steam-er came to grief, caught in a blind-ing snow- storm, she ran up on a reef.

2 Last Saturday night at twelve o'clock the steamer left the pier
She had every indication that a storm was drawing near;
With Captain Martin on the bridge she sailed that afternoon
And a hundred and thirty passengers in her steerage and saloon.

3 A blinding snowstorm did come on before she left Cape Spear.
They thought she was a powerful boat so the passengers had no fear,
While on their bunks they lay that night in calm and peaceful sleep
Not thinking before it was morning they'd be buried in the deep.

4 Up near Renews as morning dawned all hands received a shock
And as they scrambled from their berths they found they'd struck a rock;
Some rushed on deck being scarcely clad, in hopes their lives to save –
The sea soon washed them off her deck into the angry waves.

5 'She's on the rocks! She's on the rocks!' the passengers did cry.
Poor helpless women in their berths gave up their lives to die.
While strong men scrambled up in hopes their precious lives to save,
But the sea soon washed them off her decks into the angry waves.

6 Many cried and others prayed that help would be near by,
And to attract them on the shore more signals they did fly;
And soon a steamer she was seen who took them from the wreck
But only forty lives were saved from out the hundred and six.

7 A gloom was cast on every home to hear the saddening news
   About the *Florizel* went down when wrecked up near Renews;
   And ninety-four, their precious lives that evening left the shore –
   They met their doom a-drownding – we'll see them nevermore.

The *S.S. Florizel* was en route from St John's to Nova Scotia on 23 February 1918 when she
struck a reef near Renews on the southern shore of the Avalon Peninsula in a storm. The
people watching from the shore were powerless to assist the distressed ship because of the
storm's severity. Twenty-seven hours later, after the storm had calmed, a rescue was
attempted. Only 44 of the 138 people on board survived. Mrs Best learned the song from
Gerald Doyle's songbook and put her own air to it. For a detailed study of the story of the
S.S. Florizel, see Cassie Brown's *A Winter's Tale* (Toronto: Doubleday 1976).

MERCER 197

39 The Gallant Brigantine

Moses Harris
Lethbridge, 1976

As I roved on shore one eve-ning from my gal- lant
brig- an- tine to the is- land of Ja- mai--ca where I had late- ly been, so care-less- ly I
ram- bled, not car- ing where I went, down by some
rich plan-ta- tion my course I slow- ly went.

Variation (stanza 5)

5 The dress she wore it was sno-wy white, her span-ker it was green. A sil-ken shawl hung round her neck, her shoul-ders for to screen. Her hair hung down in ring-lets brown, her eyes was like the coals - She wore the face of an in-no-cent, her cheeks was like the rose.

2 The trees all 'round was decked with flowers with dark and yellow spots.
My mind being bent on roving, some melancholy thoughts;
My mind being bent on roving as I lay down to rest,
I thought on my home, my native home and the girl I love the best.

3 My people out in old Ireland they're spending their time at ease
While I am doing my foolishness ploughing the raging sea;
While I am doing my foolishness ploughing both night and day –
I will sing you a song of old Ireland to pass the cares away.

4 And when my song was finished my mind seemed more at ease.
I arose to pick some oranges that hung down from the trees;
I arose to pick some oranges that hung down by my side –
When a female form attracted me and filled me with surprise.

5 The dress she wore it was snowy white, her spanker[1] it was green.
A silken shawl round her neck her shoulders for to screen.
Her hair hung down in ringlets brown, her eyes was like the coals –
She wore the face of an innocent, her cheeks was like the rose.

6 I gently stepped up to her: 'Good morning, my fair pretty maid.'
And with a kind and gentle voice: 'Good morning, sir,' she said;
'I see you are a stranger here that lately came from sea.'
'O, yes I belong to that brigantine lies anchored in the bay.'

7 We both sot down upon the ground and chatted for awhile;
She told me of some happy hours which caused me for to smile –
And as she rose to go away unto me she said this;
'Won't you come and see my husband, he will treat you of the best.'

8 She kindly introduced me to a noble-looking man
Who modestly saluted me and took me by the hand.
The wine was on the table and dinner was served quite soon –
We three sot down together, spent a jolly good afternoon.

9 So now my song is ended, I am going to leave this land –
My name is Edward Howler, I am an Irishman.
Three years ago I leaved the shore, my troubles they began
And it's all about a fair pretty maid belonged to another man.

1 Spanker is presumably applied here to a female garment instead of a type of sail. In most variants of this song, the word is 'spencer,' a short overcoat or jacket worn by men or women.

Throughout the song Uncle Mose alternately used the two tunes given here, usually finishing on the second.
 In Dorman Ralph's version of 'The Gallant Brigantine,' he refers to Normandy in verse 3 instead of Ireland as his native home.

Singer's key D♭; MERCER 124/342

40 The *General Rawlinson*

Pius Power, Sr
Southeast Bight, 1977

Slowly

2 And she is a no- ble ves- sel as ma- ny men can tell, with eve- ry kind of fit- ting she's fit- ted out quite well; on the twen- ty-sixth of Oc- -to- ber from Ma- rys-town did steer, bound to a port called New Har- bour, caused us to be- ware.

1 Ye noble-hearted Christians I hope that you'll attend
   And listen unto those few lines that I have lately penned;
   It's concerning the *General Rawlinson* belongs to Newfoundland.
   . . .

3 Our crew was young and healthy as you may plainly see
   Willing to do their duty whatever it would be;
   To trace her jibs or reef her sails no matter how 'twould be
   Her crew was well contented when on the stormy sea.

4 We were seventeen days sailing when our skipper to us did say,
   'Have a sharp look out tonight my boys, the land is not far away;'
   He told to us the distance and brought to us good cheer,
   Being on the eighteenth morning New Harbour did appear.

5 O, now we're in New Harbour and tied up in good shape
   On the account of it being Sunday we'd have a nap of sleep;
   'Twas early Monday morning when we were called on deck
   'Twas little we thought before we'd sleep she would become a wreck.

6 O early Monday morning our orders we received,
   'Be quick and take your anchor boys and New Harbour we must leave
   To be sold up the river, our cargo for to land;'
   The wind sprang up most violently and with it hove a send.

7 We hove our anchor to the bow, our tow-line we made fast
   And owing to the heavy wind the pier she could not pass;
   The wind it blew most violently and with it hove a send
   The tug she could not take us on, we moored her up again.

8 'Twas very shortly after the wind it did die down
   And in a few more moments it did chop right around;
   It pitched a gale from the west-north-west and blew most violently
   Which caused our vessel to go ashore with mourners there for we.

9 We then bent our big anchor and we threw it o'er her rail
   We were intended to hold her on in that tremendous gale;
   We held her on for a short while but proved to be in vain
   Our hawser it had parted and we were adrift again.

10 'Twas very shortly after, the vessel struck the rocks
   The breaking seas broke over her she got some heavy knocks.
   'Look out my boys,' our skipper cries, 'we cannot do no more,'
   And with the help of a smaller boat got landed safe on shore.

11 O now we're safely landed and new lodgings to go seek
   We were placed in a restaurant where we have spent three weeks,
   . . .
   When sour wine we had for tea and half enough to eat.

12 At eight o'clock in the morning it's coffee you'll receive
   A half a slice of bread with that our appetite to feed;
   A bowl of soup for dinner and that not very nice,
   A couple o' picks of meat in that, and two spoonfuls of rice.

13 You'll get the same for supper as all our crew can tell
And we were not used to rationing, we were not feeling well;
The *Molly and Jacob* she came in and plenty we received –
You bet we were not sorry when New Harbour we did leave.

14 O now I'm on my way for home I got no more to tell
But some fine day in summer I'll word it for a friend;
I'll word it for a friend of mine and if he thinks 'twill do
We'll learn it off and to our mate he'll sing it for the crew.

The *General Rawlinson*, built in Marystown, was in the charge of Captain James Harris on a voyage to Oporto in Portugal in 1921-2. While at New Harbour on 7 January during the return voyage, the *Rawlinson* tied up to await good weather. However, the wind grew stronger causing the ship's anchors to drag. The *Rawlinson* struck against the dock, took on water, and sank. She was raised in July 1922 and eventually sold to be used by the Portuguese (renamed *Pacos de Brando*) as a Bank fishing vessel.

The *General Rawlinson* was composed by Mr Ben Doucey of Marystown. Since the first verse is incomplete, we have used the second with the music.

Singer's key A♭

41 George Alfred Beckett

Moses Harris
Lethbridge, 1976

Slowly

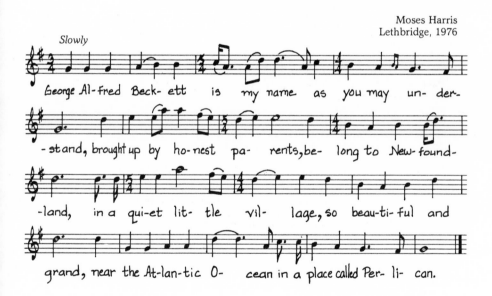

George Al-fred Beck-ett is my name as you may un-der-
-stand, brought up by ho-nest pa-rents, be-long to New-found-
-land, in a qui-et lit-tle vil-lage, so beau-ti-ful and
grand, near the At-lan-tic O-cean in a place called Per-li-can.

71

2 My parents reared me tenderly, the truth I will make known;
   And good advice they give to me when I was leaving home.
   My mother prayed for my return as she often did before;
   As I leaved home that day to roam far from my native shore.

3 To the coal fields of Cape Breton my course I soon did stray,
   All for to seek employment I landed in Glace Bay;
   (It's little did my mother know when she bid me good-bye,
   What country I might travel in or what death I might die.)

4 One evening last summer as you may understand,
   For to drive out the Tower Road, I engaged a taximan;
   But little he knew as we rode on, I had an iron bar,
   Those dreadful wounds for to inflict, and rob him in his car.

5 From the scene I made my quick escape, for to get home was my plan,
   I leaved Glace Bay and sailed away back home to Newfoundland;
   In less than three weeks after, the police was on my trail,
   I was arrested for this murder and brought back to St John's jail.

6 From that back to Cape Breton, my trial for to stand,
   And never more to see again my own dear native land;
   And not forgetting my dear wife wherever she may be,
   O loving, kind, and gentle, the fault was all with me.

From the information I have gathered, it seems the murder described in this song took place in Glace Bay, Nova Scotia, shortly before Christmas of 1930. George Alfred Beckett was tried in Glace Bay on 5 January 1931, for the murder of Nicolas Marthos and again on 21 February 1931 and was sentenced to hang on 20 April. Apparently, this was the last public hanging in Sydney.

In a version of the song as sung by Marsella and John James Whitty of North Sydney and collected by Ronnie MacEachern, the last two lines of the sixth verse are:

The jury found me guilty and the judge made this reply
On the thirtieth day of April for this murder you must die.

There are also two additional verses in their rendition of the song:

My life is almost to an end, my days are just a few
Take my advice and happy live and avoid all troubles too;
But never murder anyone whatever you may do
Or like me you'll die on the gallows at the age of forty-two.

And now for to conclude and finish from this world I must part
For the murder of Nicolas Martyrs will leave me sorry to the heart;
So let all of you take warning and remember what I say
And may the Lord have mercy on my soul after I pass away.

The lines within parentheses in the third verse are also taken from this version.

Singer's key A^b

42 The *Gigantic*

Pius Power, Sr
Southeast Bight, 1978

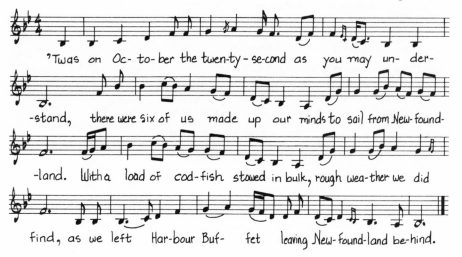

'Twas on Oc-to-ber the twen-ty-se-cond as you may un-der-stand, there were six of us made up our minds to sail from New-found-land. With a load of cod-fish stowed in bulk, rough wea-ther we did find, as we left Har-bour Buf-fet leaving New-found-land be-hind.

2　As we left Harbour Buffet I'm sure all hands inclined,
　　The wind sprang up 'bout east-north-east, we had a splendid time;
　　In under a foresail and two jibs, Red Island we did round,
　　Sailing out through Placentia Bay, for Oporto we were bound.

3　'Bout eight o'clock on that same night, this light it did appear
　　Cape St Mary's on a beam, southeast from us did bear.
　　We ran her out around the Keys, our sails and sheets we bound,
　　And bore across 'bout south-by-east, expecting to veer down.

4　'Twas early the next morning Cape Pine it did appear.
　　The light it was 'bout east-north-east and south-by-east we steered.
　　We set our stormsail to the mast, and that was done right well.
　　We changed the watch at eight o'clock, the time it struck eight bells.

5　We set the log at ten o'clock, and slacked it back astern.
　　We ran her off across the seas 'til early the next morn.
　　We hauled the log at eleven o'clock, the course was given then,
　　Eighty-one was on her log, so we swung her off again.

6　Southeast-by-east was our main course, but south-by-east she lay
　　Owing to the weather, and according to the sea.
　　We runned her off for ten long hours, the wind was on the veer,
　　Our captain says to haul her in, southeast-by-east to steer.

7　Now running off southeast-by-east, the gale it did come on.
　　Our captain cried: 'All hands on deck, and that before too long!'
　　We lowered our staysails from the mast, four of our jolly crew
　　Reefed foresail and reefed stormsail and then hove our vessel to.

8   It was on October the twenty-fourth, as you may understand,
    We shortened sail and hove her to, three hundred miles from land.
    The night being dark and dreary, a hard time we did spend.
    A sea rolled down on our lifeboat, split her from end to end.

9   From four to eight we did go around the lanyards we did view
    That is a job that must be done, when a vessel is hove to
    To serve the lines and keep her pumped, as you may understand
    Three hundred jogs unto an hour far off from Newfoundland.

10 The twenty-eight hours that we lay to, in the west edge of Gulf Stream
    The wind and seas that were sent forth, the like was seldom seen,
    Four sailor boys to stand the watch that night and livelong day,
    And six o'clock on Saturday night we ran before the sea.

11 On the last day of October we hove her to again –
    In under a two-reef foresail a hard old night to spend.
    With a knot tied in her stormsail and a reef put in likewise,
    We stood on deck that livelong night with salt water in our eyes.

12 From eight to twelve our watch came on as you may plainly see.
    It would bring the tears to weep to look upon the sea,
    To see those waves come rolling down, we could do nothing more –
    We hove her to on Thursday night, off of a foreign shore.

13 And now the gale is over and is coming to an end –
    We won't forget the thirty-first and the hard time we did spend
    Down in the North Atlantic those raging seas to fight,
    And us young boys will never forget the seas rolled down that night.

14 Next morning we lay in the calm, a whistle we did hear.
    We took the tug, made fast our lines, for land, sure, we did steer.
    For twenty-three days and twenty-three nights we were on the ocean deep.
    We furled her sails and washed her down and took a nap of sleep.

15 'Twas five miles up the river our load we did discharge;
    One half our fish was small, my boys, the other half was large.
    We took aboard our load of salt, on San Antonia's strand,
    And with good health all sails were sot, bound home for Newfoundland.

16 Six men composed the schooner's crew – their names I will pen down:
    Captain Thomas Edgecombe of Catalina town,
    And William Edgecombe he was mate, a smart young man he being,
    And William Best from Placentia Bay, hailing from Merasheen.

17 Wilson Hollett was our steward's name from Buffet do belong,
    And Thomas Whiffen from The Rams, I'll have him in my song;
    And William Barry from Port Royal made up the schooner's crew –
    As we shipped on board the *Gigantic* to sail the ocean blue.

The *Gigantic* was composed in 1917 by William Best of Merasheen, my father's uncle. Mrs Mary Best, my father's aunt, gave me this copy of her brother's song. I have heard it sung several times, but never in its entirety. It is interesting to note that the song underwent various textual changes as it was passed from singer to singer, community to community. It was generally a 'man's' song, sung at gatherings of men drinking a drop of homebrew on a winter's evening. A.B.

The *Glen Alone*

43 The *Glen Alone*

Pius Power, Sr
Southeast Bight, 1983

It's on-ly a ri-vel[1] and just a puff that's mov-ing her old brown sail, like a sick-(e)-ly man with a fe-ver and faint she mutters a-while and stays; in a short while af-ter the wind it died, and she rolled on the oil-y sea, like a sick-(e)-ly man with a fe-ver and faint she was mov-ing un-eas-i-ly.

2 There ain't no stir in our old barque now, she might have been a log –
   Three leagues away and the land lay low in a cold, grey bank of fog;
   About three points on her starboard bow one summer's night in June,
   Where the sky and the water seemed joined in one, lit up with a brightful
   moon.

3 Through bloody reds and silvery stars on a faint and a glorious night,
   Straight from our barque to the ocean stood our wavering, burning lights;
   There's something in that shiny bank about one league away –
   Like the dreary form of a stoutish rock on the face of the water lay.

4 There ain't no rock in my east line now, in my chart not here about –
   I looked through my night-glass steadily but I could not make it out;
   I fixed my eye on that ugly form 'til it passed by our quarter-deck,
   And I ordered the crew to lower a boat for maybe it is a wreck.

5 We rowed aboard that ugly form as it stood in the light of the moon –
   I read from the bow of that mystic barque her strange name, *Glen Alone*;
   We hailed them but never a word was spoke, there was no one on her deck.
   We unshipped our oars, attached her side, and climbed aboard the wreck.

6 Through rugged yards and splintered spars, her mainmast and mizzen gone –
There's scattered boats on her blizzard[2] deck, but human forms were none;
Until we saw one human form was crouched upon her deck,
With an old sou'wester and guernsey on, shipmate, one of the wreck.

7 I gently raised that old chap's hat, I remember the moon was full –
I was starting aft when the light fell on his glimmering, ghostly skull;
In starting aft the deck seemed flushed, all muddled with shady lights,
And six more skeletons there we found all bleached to a dawny white.

8 Through rugged yards and splintered spars to her cabin we then made way –
Stretched on the locker in full length her skeleton captain lay;
And in his bony fingers he held the note I read next day –
'Shipwrecked we are and our food all gone, we pray and fade away.'

9 O we rowed away from that ugly form as she stood against the moon –
I read from the bow of that mystic barque once more, the *Glen Alone*;
When faster and faster into the deep the blade of our stout oars fell –
Her deck seemed swarmed with shadows and cries a-bidding their last
farewell.

10 I will never look out of my night-glass again by the pitiful light of the moon –
But I'll think on the horrors we once performed in the wreck of the *Glen
Alone*!

1 Rivel is possibly the result of a sound change; its standard equivalent would be ripple.
This alternation of p/b to v is common in certain Newfoundland dialects and can be
heard in other words such as 'scrivel' for scribble.
2 Blizzard, according to Mr Power, means flat or even.

Mr Power learned this song from Mr George Follett in the 1920s when Mr Follett was in
his seventies.

44 The *Glenora*

Margaret Carroll
Ramea, 1977

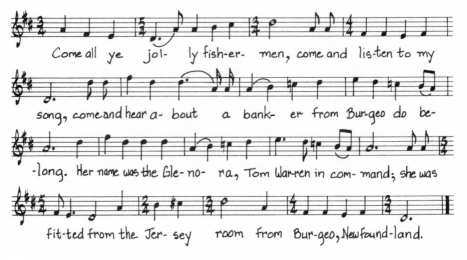

Come all ye jol-ly fish-er-men, come and lis-ten to my song, come and hear a-bout a bank-er from Bur-geo do be-long. Her name was the Gle-no-ra, Tom Warren in com-mand; she was fit-ted from the Jer-sey room from Bur-geo, Newfound-land.

2 She carried a crew of six brave men and dories she had two –
. . .
They all belonged to Burgeo, each all of (whom) you know well
And they damn nigh met a dirty end in one heavy northeast gale.

3 On the sixteenth day of April the *Nora* she set sail –
Bound for the banks of Scotland to set another trawl;
The wind sprang up from the east-north-east and around the head did roar –
As God should have it on that day, Tom Warren he stayed on shore.

4 And when they had their trawl set, they shaped her for the land,
The wind sprang up quite suddenly but nothing could she stand;
They tried to beat her in Cannoire when her double reefs gave way
And going into Galliboy 'twas aloft and bear away.

5 And on that following Friday morn the wind it did die out –
Tom Warren got in his motor boat the *Nora* to find out.
With Friday morning passed away and evening coming on
The *Glenora* sailed into Muddy Hole with double-reef foresail gone.

6 And when they sailed into Muddy Hole, Captain Tom was at the wheel,
'Let run your jib he loudly roared, your jumbo too, as well;
And then let run your foresail while she is shooting slow –
And then cocks-bill your anchor all ready to let go.'

7 And when the anchor it runned down, sure it was nearly dark –
Captain Tom gave orders what must be done before it did come dark:
And now my boys do not forget be sure and set the pump.'
'Twas skipper Tom he sidled aft and crawled into his bunk.

8　And then they cleared for sea again if the *Nora* she will stand –
　　They carried the same skipper, Tom Warren all in command.
　　At four o'clock that evening the *Nora* hove in sight,
　　At six o'clock that evening they anchored her all right.

9　And now my song is to an end, to you I'll sing no more –
　　Tom Warren is off to the western ground from Scotland to Cannoire.
　　And I swear a man like Skipper Tom his head is rather large;
　　And between the sense and the foolishness, I don't think he should have
　　　charge!

Although I was not able to determine the exact location of the Banks of Scotland, Mr Clyde Rose informs me that they are somewhere in the Burgeo area off the Southwest Coast where as a boy growing up he remembers hearing people speak of local fishing banks called the Banks of Scotland. The other place names referred to in the song are also in the Burgeo area.

45 Grá Geal Mo Chroí

Philip Foley
Tilting, 1980

2　I promised to marry this innocent dove
　　All by a fond letter saying she was my love –
　　Expecting that evening some pleasures to see
　　Or a token of love from sweet grá geal mo chroí.

3　But this great roguish villyan whom I did entrust
　　Of all men of letters I'm sure he's the worst.
　　He proved a deceiver and a traitor to me,
　　He ne'er gave my letter to grá geal mo chroí.

79

4 He have it to her father as I understand.
   He immediately reached him the letter in hand,
   And the moment he read it he swore bitterly
   He'd alter accord with sweet grá geal mo chroí.

5 He called down his daughter with scorn and disdain
   Saying: 'Here is a letter from your darling swain.
   You cannot deny it, it's plain for to see
   He titles you here his sweet grá geal mo chroí.'

6 This innocent damsel she fell on her knees
   Saying: 'Honoured aged father, you may do as you please,
   Though it's between horses tortured I'll be,
   I'll never deny I'm his grá geal mo chroí.'

7 A coach was made ready that very same day
   And far from this country my love sent away.
   I'm searching the country, this wide world all 'round
   From seaport to seaport and can't find her out.

8 (I'll travel this wide world, I'll cruise it all 'round
   And perhaps in some part my love may be found,)
   But if I don't find her, I'll mourn constantly,
   My last dying words will be grá geal mo chroí!

The Irish words 'grá geal mo chroí,' meaning 'bright love of my heart,' are usually written in English as 'Grogal McCree' to give an idea of the pronunciation. Mr Foley knew exactly what the words meant. Songs of this type reflect a strong Irish tradition in Tilting, where Mr Foley comes from, a small Irish-Newfoundland community on Fogo Island in Notre Dame Bay.

   The first two lines in the last verse were taken from another version of the song since they were not provided by Mr Foley.

MERCER 110

46 The Grand Falls Tragedy

Bride Rose
Placentia, 1975

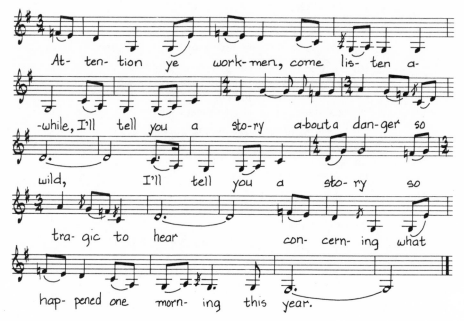

At- ten- tion ye work-men, come lis- ten a-
-while, I'll tell you a sto-ry a-bout a dan-ger so
wild, I'll tell you a sto- ry so
tra- gic to hear con- cern- ing what
hap- pened one morn- ing this year.

2 Concerning what happened one day in our town,
  When three busy workmen were by death stricken down;
  While the rest of us slumbered and all things so still –
  This accident happened not far from the mill.

3 This accident happened around three o'clock,
  When three in a flat-car (that) had been laden with rocks;
  Fell down an incline, plunged fifty feet deep –
  Far down in the rock-cut those men were asleep.

4 'Twas little they knew that the blocks in support –
  (And this was the story the newspaper told)
  The rock-laden flat-car somehow had become free,
  And dashed down the railroad with the greatest of speed.

5 Those three men were injured who toiled unaware
  (Of) the oncoming monster bringing death to them there;
  There were quickly and sadly from the earth snatched away –
  They were toiling that morning where the great danger lay.

6 Attention ye workmen, come list' one and all –
  The names of those workmen I now will recall;
  The first one was Marshall from old Carbonear,
  Who died far from home boys, and loved ones so dear.

7 The second was Tobin who met a sad doom,
  As he toiled that morning when all was in bloom;
  For he was a native of Ship Cove they say –
  And sad was the tidings that went out that day.

8 The third helpless victim was young William All [*sic*]
  He belonged to the town boys, well-known to us all;
  He were just a young fellow, a lad of nineteen –
  Sure, the blow to his parents it must have fell keen.

9 Far down in the rock-cut so deep and so wide,
  Those men toiled together each day side by side;
  Of death never dreaming nor dangerous ways –
  When suddenly death stared them each one in the face.

10 On Friday night boys, the express came through,
   With passengers loaded and all of her crew;
   Those bodies were taken and put on the train,
   Back home to be carried where sorrow did reign.

11 My story is ended, I have no more to say.
   Those three stricken workmen now sleep 'neath the clay;
   There God will keep them until we all meet,
   In the great Resurrection in heaven so sweet.

I first heard this song one night when my Uncle Mack and I were visiting Mrs Bride (it is customary in Newfoundland to use Christian names, for both men and women, together with the title of marital status). Uncle Mack enjoyed the song enormously; every so often during a pause in the singing he would interject 'Good Woman!' or 'Well done!' Mrs Bride learned the song 'off a paper' and put her own air to it. When I asked her if she had composed the air she said, 'I can't remember – I might have.' A.B.

47 The Green Mossy Banks of the Lea

Edward Ward
Southeast Bight, 1975

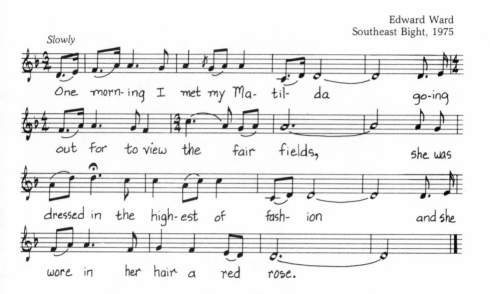

One morning I met my Matilda going out for to view the fair fields, she was dressed in the highest of fashion and she wore in her hair a red rose.

2 I stepped up and bid her good morning,
Her cheeks they did blush like a rose;
Saying; 'Fair maid while the meadows are charming
Your guider I'll be if you choose.'

3 'Kind sir I don't need any guider –
Young man you're a stranger to me;
Look yonder my father is coming
O'er the green mossy banks of the lea.'

4 He waited 'til up came her father
To cheer up his spirits once more –
Saying: 'Kind sir, if this is your daughter
She's the charming, sweet girl I adore.

5 Five thousand a year is my fortune
And a lady your daughter will be;
She can ride in her coach every morning
O'er the green mossy banks of the lea.'

6 Come all ye fair, pretty maids take warning
No matter how poor you may be –
Be gentle like this young Matilda
O'er the green mossy banks of the lea.

This song appears in other collections with more complete texts than the version given here. However, the air is quite different from the others that I have seen, and because of its beautiful musical qualities I have included Edward Ward's rendition. The other versions have the following as the first two verses:

When first to this country a stranger,
Curiosity caused me to roam,
Over Ireland in exile I wandered,
Far from my American home.

Till at length I arrived in sweet Erin,
In my land where I longs to be,
My footsteps were guided by fairies,
On the green mossy banks of the lea.

MERCER 128

48 Gull Cove

Pius Power
Southeast Bight, 1979

2 It happened to be in the summertime in the lovely month of June,
   When the birds were gaily singing and the meadows were in full bloom;
   Our schooner we got ready, to prosecute did go
   The codfish down in Gull Cove, where the stormy winds do blow.

3 From Placentia Bay we sailed away, I do mean Petit Fort.
   Our fishing gear was codtraps a voyage for to bring forth;
   But if the codfish fades away as it often done before,
   We could lose our year in Gull Cove, where the stormy winds do blow.

4 O the first few days that we were there the weather it proved fine –
And when the next ones rolled along, well, they're another kind;
Our hawsers we got ready and we had to let them go –
And we sailed away from Gull Cove, where the stormy winds do blow.

5 We runned her to St Mary's, it was a place of rest –
Particularly up in Riverhead, that's where we all love best;
But when the gale is over, back to our gear we'll go –
To the rugged shores of Gull Cove, where the stormy winds do blow.

6 When we arrived at Gull Cove, everything it did look grum –
Our traps lay in good order, also our skiff and all;
There's no sign of fish meshed in our twine, and well we all do know
That we'll make the skunk [*sic*] in Gull Cove, where the stormy winds do
    blow.

7 The schooner the *Madonna Hayden* and Tommy in command –
He always got a saving voyage since he came to Gull Cove strand;
But the spring when he was leaving home, he had no mind to go
To the rugged shores in Gull Cove, where the stormy winds do blow.

8 O the *James and Mary Hayden* is riding up ahead –
And the other day when Captain Jim unto his men he said:
'There's no better sign today my boys than there was a month ago;
O the curse o' Hell on Gull Cove, where the stormy winds do blow.'

9 Bill Emberley from Spencer's Cove in the schooner the *Village Bride* –
He is anchored down in Gull Cove, out on the foaming tide.
If he had gone to the Southern Shore, he might have got a load,
But he'll lose his year in Gull Cove, where the stormy winds do blow.

10 My song it only reaches up as far as Ladder Cove point –
They might be getting fish up there, but the boats looks very buoyant;
They might be getting fish up there, and they don't want us to know –
And we are down in Gull Cove, where the stormy winds do blow.

11 The *Carrie and Aggie Bailey* I do mean Patrick Hann,
'Tis now he is lamenting, but it's all in God's command;
God's holy will it must be done and well we all do know,
We will lose our year in Gull Cove, where the stormy winds do blow.

12 For myself, the great composer, it makes no odds to me,
I have a good time sleeping, there's nothing to trouble me;
But when my meals are cooked and et, back to my berth I'll go –
And the Gull Cove waves lulls me asleep, where the stormy winds do blow.

13 Now to conclude and finish, I do mean to end my song,
My name is Matty Johnston, to Petit Forte I do belong;
I don't think I've offended you, so far forth as I know –
But I'll bid adieu to Gull Cove, where the stormy winds do blow.

Gull Cove is near Branch, St Mary's Bay. Mr Power learned the song from 'the fellow who made it' in the 1920s.

49 Heave Away!

Pius Power, Sr
Southeast Bight, 1979

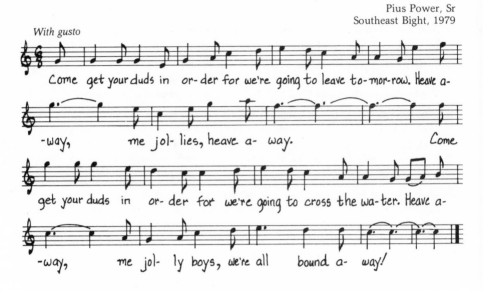

With gusto

Come get your duds in or-der for we're going to leave to-mor-row. Heave a-way, me jol-lies, heave a-way. Come get your duds in or-der for we're going to cross the wa-ter. Heave a-way, me jol-ly boys, we're all bound a-way!

2 Sometimes we're bound for Liverpool,
  More times we're bound for Spain.
  Chorus: Heave away, me jollies, heave away
  But now we're bound for St John's town
  To watch the girls dancing.
  Chorus: Heave away, me jolly boys, we're all bound away!

3 And 'tis farewell Maggie darling,
  For it's now I'm going to leave you.
  Chorus: Heave away, me jollies, heave away
  I promised that I'd marry you
  But how I did deceive you!
  Chorus: Heave away me jolly boys, we're all bound away!

4 I wrote me a love letter
  And I signed it with a ring.
  Chorus: Heave away, me jollies, heave away
  I wrote me love a letter
  I was on the *Jenny Lind.*
  Chorus: Heave away, me jolly boys, we're all bound away!

5 Sometimes we're bound for Liverpool,
  More times we're bound for Spain.
  Chorus: Heave away, me jollies, heave away
  But now we're bound for St John's town
  To watch the girls dancing.
  Chorus: Heave away, me jolly boys, we're all bound away!

This is a song which was often used to establish a rhythm for hauling up the anchors aboard the fishing schooners. Many of these 'heave-up shanties' were old ballads or contemporary ones, and very often topical verses were made up on the spur of the moment and added to the song to make the song last as long as the task itself.
  In the third verse, it is sometimes Maggie who does the deceiving.

50 The Herring

Ernest Barter
Ramea, 1977

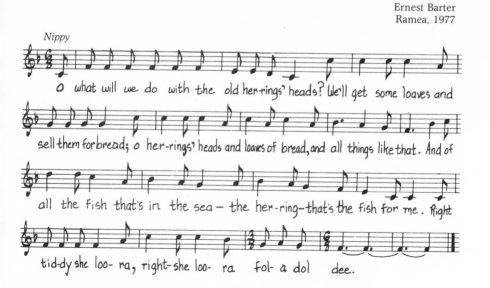

Nippy

O what will we do with the old her-rings' heads? We'll get some loaves and sell them for bread; o her-rings' heads and loaves of bread, and all things like that. And of all the fish that's in the sea — the her-ring — that's the fish for me. Right tid-dy she loo-ra, right-she loo-ra fol-a dol dee.

2 O what will we do with the old herrings' eyes?
   We'll get some puddings and sell them for pies;
   O herrings' eyes, puddings for pies
   Herrings' heads and loaves for bread, and all things like that.
   And of all the fish that's in the sea
   The herring that's the fish for me –
   Right tiddy she loo-ra, right-she loo-ra, fol-a dol dee.

3 O what will we do with the old herrings' fins?
   We'll get some needles and sell them for pins;
   Herrings' fins and needles for pins
   Herrings' eyes, puddings and pies
   Herrings' heads and loaves for bread, and all things like that.
   And of all the fish that's in the sea
   The herring that's the fish for me –
   Right tiddy she loo-ra, right-she loo-ra, fol-a dol dee.

4 O what will we do with the old herrings' backs?
   We'll get a little boy and call him Jack;
   O herrings' backs, boys called Jack
   Herrings' fins and needles for pins
   Herrings' eyes, puddings and pies
   Herrings' heads and loaves for bread, and all things like that.
   And of all the fish that's in the sea
   The herring that's the fish for me –
   Right tiddy she loo-ra, right-she loo-ra, fol-a dol dee.

5 O what will we do with the old herrings' bellies?
   We'll get a little girl and call her Nellie;
   O herrings' bellies and girls called Nellie
   Herrings' backs, boys called Jack
   Herrings' fins and needles for pins
   Herrings' eyes, puddings and pies
   Herrings' heads and loaves for bread, and all things like that.
   And of all the fish that's in the sea
   The herring that's the fish for me –
   Right tiddy she loo-ra, right-she loo-ra, fol-a dol dee.

6 O what will we do with the old herrings' scales?
   We'll get some canvas and sew it for sails;
   O herrings' scales, canvas for sails
   Herrings' bellies and girls called Nellie
   Herrings' backs, boys called Jack
   Herrings' fins and needles for pins
   Herrings' eyes, puddings and pies
   Herrings' heads and loaves for bread, and all things like that.
   And of all the fish that's in the sea
   The herring that's the fish for me –
   Right tiddy she loo-ra, right-she loo-ra, fol-a dol dee.

'The Herring' song comes from a late eighteenth-century broadsheet, 'The Fishes'
Lamentation,' subtitled 'A New Song.' It seems the song originally contained allusions to
the idea that the herring, being the king of the fish, was the embodiment of some ancient,

regeneration ritual. However, the song has since been modified somewhat and, according to Mr Barter, his version was very often sung to children. Uncle Mose knew the song as the 'Jolly Jack Herring':

O what do you think of me jolly jack herring,
He's forty feet wide and he's fifty feet long –
To me E so and I so and E cock a lair E-o
Why didn't you told me so?
So I did long ago
Very well, then, don't you think I done well with me jolly jack herring?

51 The Hoban Boys

Pius Power, Sr
Southeast Bight, 1976

At- ten- tion, all ye coun- try- men, and lis- ten to my song, I hope ye'll pay at- -ten- tion, I'll not de- lay you long; I hope ye'll pay at- ten- tion to what I got to say 'bout a loss we had to suf- fer from a dread- ful north- east gale.

2 'Twas on October the twenty-sixth, the day before the gale –
When we were still a-fishing, our courage didn't fail.
The bait being very plentiful, and the weather acting fine
And for to have another set we all felt well inclined.

89

3 We took our seine in dory for to have a row along;
   We rowed around the island and plenty of herring found.
   We payed away our seine, my boys, those scaly fish did get –
   But the loss we came to after, I never will forget.

4 'Twas early next morning those three boats left the bar –
   They're bound out for Oderin's bank, the distance wasn't far;
   The gale sprang up tremendously, they were forced to set inside
   And in under close-reefed canvas to the harbour we arrived.

5 The first come in was Hobans', their hawser it was low –
   They says: 'We'll anchor on the bar for in she cannot go.'
   The next come in was Robert Deer, he wasn't far behind;
   He anchored just astern of us and put ashore a line.

6 The next come in was Peavy, all in the smallest boat –
   He anchored just astern of him and put ashore a rope;
   Said one unto the other: 'I think it's to its side,
   If it don't blow any harder they'll be all right here tonight.'

7 At ten o'clock that very night it blew a hurricane –
   At daybreak in the morning, not one was to be seen;
   They must have swept their anchor, the truth to you I'll tell,
   God only knows where these boats are, not one of us can tell.

8 At ten o'clock that very day the wind it did die down –
   The *Minnie* she was sighted and high and dry on ground;
   On Woody Island's western point it caused her bones to crack,
   She was scrubbed and tore to pieces and she there became a wreck. [1]

9 The owners of the other two they still got no report –
   Some thinks they're on the bottom, but they could be still afloat;
   The very next news that reached our ears gave us a dreadful shock,
   The *Lilly* and *Jim* was sighted, sunk at the harbour rock.

10 We then made haste and went to her expecting her to sail –
   But still she is a total loss and met a watery grave;
   We saved her spars and bowsprit but nothing more could do,
   By the help of those Oderin men and Little Harbour, too.

11 In turning from that dreadful wreck a message we did hear –
   The other boat she was picked up and towed in at St Pierre;
   Her owners are the Hoban boys and the *Mayflower* is her name
   Through French and English councillors we'll get our boat again.

12 We hastened to the office a message for to send –
   To see how much 'twould cost us to get her from French hands.
   The message then that we received, and we were glad to hear
   The *Argyle* or the *Daisy* would take us to St Pierre.

13 But we received another since the government proved false –
   The *Argyle* or the *Daisy* don't come to our sad loss.
   But still there is another chance that we can get along;
   Our loyal friend is Henry Lake, I'll have him in the song.

14 O now we're ready for the start to sail unto St Pierre –
    Our whole intention is the boat and to try to get our gear;
    But when we reached St Peter the French to us did say:
    'There's one hundred and fifty dollars boys, before she leaves the quay.'

15 Besides our boat she had been robbed of caplin, dory, too –
    They also tried to sink her when on the sea so blue;
    The chops they made with a fatal axe, I'll show you any time
    She have it on her starboard side right at the water line.

16 O now we leaved that funny place, St Pierre a long ways behind –
    Bound to a port of entry with everything going fine;
    When we gets through the Customs it's straight for home we'll go
    And we'll lower her in the harbour where northeasters they can't blow.

17 When we gets in the harbour we'll drink our drop of rum –
    For Christmas it is handy, and I'm sure we'll have some fun.
    We'll soon forget the hardships that we did undergo
    When sailing for the *Mayflower* in bitter frost and snow.

18 O now my song is to an end and don't you think it true –
    But if you thinks I'm telling you lies you ask some of the crew.
    I think I done my very best, I know it can be beat
    For it concerns that northeast gale, October the twenty-eighth.

1 Wreck is pronounced wrack to rhyme with crack.

This very lengthy and involved story of storm, wreck, and subsequent salvage was
apparently composed by Bill Hoban, one of the owners of the *Mayflower*, in the 1920s. Mr
Power learned it from his uncle, John Power, who learned it from the composer.

The Hole in the Wall

52 The Hole in the Wall

Pius Power, Sr
Southeast Bight, 1980

Steady swing

Ye lads and ye las-ses, I pray pay at- ten-tion and lis-ten a-

-while un-to what I will tell; con- cern-ing a

dance that we had here last Sun-day, I ad-ded those ver-ses to

make it go well. On Sat-ur-day night when all

hands was in- vit- ed to be there on Sun-day to o- pen a

ball, in a sad-dle-roofed house – no names I will

men-tion – I'll ti- tle the har-bour the Hole in the Wall.

2 At noon on a Sunday where the crowd they did gather,
The lands and the lasses their young hearts was gay;
Linked into each other they jogged on together,
Through bog-holes and marshes they all made their way.
O I being a stranger so I followed after,
It being my first time on those high roads you know;
There's one in particular I took as a pilot
That travelled those same roads a few years ago.

3 As soon as we reached there the music was playing –
   Well, scarce had it sounded when the dance did begin;
   I knew by the first glance the girls they were plenty,
   I think they could average about two a man.
   Said I to my friend; 'Boy, is this a theatre?'
   I'll never forget all what sights I have seen;
   I thought them so marvellous with their gold belts and bracelets,
   Their tiny silk dresses just under their knees.

4 Said I to my friend: 'Boy, they are the first type,
   And they'll all go at medium, there's none of them small.'
   There's one in particular, her name I will mention –
   And that is fair Flora, the pride of them all.
   I said: 'Now fair Flora, don't you be offended,
   And if you are, your pardon I'll make;
   You are neat and handsome, your figure most gorgeous –
   I know there's a two-buckle spring in your leg.'

5 We danced there that evening, we left all contented,
   And the far-away girls they got anxious for home;
   And some of those boys they are very restless –
   They left them to climb up the hills all alone.
   There's one lass among us was late on arriving –
   She must have met weather and had to go in;
   I heard great inquiry was made by her owner,
   That she was too late to get tea for the men.

6 I listened awhile to their low conversation –
   You'd want to be smart if you'd answer their plan;
   I laughed at the idea, such small information,
   I says to myself: 'You called up the wrong man.'
   But now I'll conclude and I'll finish my ditty,
   My mind is tormented, no more can I rhyme;
   And if you're offended, your temper I'll mend it –
   I might find a three-leg someday I get time!

'The Hole in the Wall' refers to the village of Little Bona in Placentia Bay. Mr Peter Leonard composed the song about a dance there one night. Mr Power accompanied him to the dance; the song was made up either that night or very shortly after. In no time at all everybody was singing it.

Singer's key A♭; MERCER 133

53 The Huntingdown Shore

Pius Power, Sr
Southeast Bight, 1977

Moderate, free swing

We shipped with young Good-ridge in the spring of the year, and we got thir-ty shil-lings to find our own gear; thirty shil-lings in hand and good tea in ga-lore, and four meals a day on the Hunt-ing-down shore.

2 On the fourteenth of June our two anchors we weighed,
And the order for sailing was not long delayed;
Consigned unto Goodridge to Hunt and LeMore,
Who sends the men fishing on Huntingdown shore.

3 The first night at sea we met a great squall;
We let go our royals, our topsails and all.
We shortened our sail, and we couldn't do more,
And then took our course for the Huntingdown shore.

4 Men, women, and children they lay on their backs,
While more in their bunks, they were straightened like sacks;
And more lay on boxes, their sides they were sore,
They longed to be landed on the Huntingdown shore.

5 'Twas early next morning just at break of day,
We arose from our slumber and got underway;
Put bread in the cuddy, and pork on the floor,
And shaped her for fishing on the Huntingdown shore.

6 We kept aft the sheets and kept her full and by,
With the wind from the sou'west as close as she'd lie;
'Til we came to Hare Island, then straightway we bore,
And safely we anchored near Huntingdown shore.

7 We put out our lines then, our luck there to find,
Every man in the boat sure for fishing inclined;
We cooked but three meals, but I'm sure we'd want more,
And then we hauled up and left Huntingdown shore.

8 The girls on Round Island on us they did smile,
   Saying: 'Here is young Cormack, young Keefe, and young Doyle;
   They are three great strangers on the Labrador,
   We have lately arrived up from Huntingdown shore.'

9 Now, as for Round Island, the truth I will tell,
   No one who goes on it but loves it right well.
   It is a fine harbour on the Labrador,
   But it can't be compared with the Huntingdown shore.

10 'Tis true I'm a toper – that's very well known,
   If I saved what I earned, I might live at home.
   In drink and carousing I spent all my store,
   Which makes me lament on the Huntingdown shore.

According to Gerald S. Doyle, 'The Huntingdown Shore' was composed in the 1860s by a
St John's fisherman named Doyle. Goodridge's was one of the mercantile establishments of
that period. The Huntingdown or Huntingdon shore was a fishing area on the Labrador
coast.

MERCER 134

54 Hush-oh-bye Baby

Kitty O'Shaugnessy
Kingman's Cove, 1974

Plaintively

As I ro-vèd out on a cold win-ter's eve-ning, down by a large for-est I hap-pened to stray, being ful-ly in-ten-ded to vis-it a neigh-bour 'til I was pre-ven-ted by cold, hea-vy rain. The wind it blew high and tre-men-dous-ly sleet-ing. I sat my-self down be-neath a large tree, when to my sur-prise I heard some-bo-dy speak-ing, re-peat-ing those words, crying: "Hush-o-bye, ba-by."

2 I being confounded, with close shades surrounded
   I drew a little nigh to see what it might be;
   What should I see but a poor, distressed woman
   With a babe in her arms and two on her knee.
   'O Heavens!' she cried. 'Is there no consolation,
   Or is there no reason in humanity?
   My children are sleeping, they'll cry if they're wakened –
   O hush-oh-by baby, hush-oh-bye baby.'

3 I said: 'My good woman were you ever married,
   Or where is the father of your children small?
   Have you no home or no house to reside in,
   Or if you were wealthy, what caused your downfall?'
   'Oh, yes, kind sir, I own I was married
   To one who is buried, it's plain to be seen;
   All I can say, sir, it all proved in vain, for
   They gave me the road to sing hush-oh-bye baby.

4 It's seven long years since we both met together
   And married we were with our parent's consent.
   We lived in a place they called Newtown Perry,
   And never 'til now had I cause to lament.
   Until the twenty-ninth day of last March he was going
   Out in his farm his cattle to see;
   'Twas little he thought he would never return
   To hear his poor wife crying hush-oh-bye baby.

5 As he was a-driving along through the city
   A large crowd of people he happened to see.
   Some holy, some human [sic] with guns and firearms,
   And likewise a large gang of the peasantry.
   Little he thought of their wicked intentions,
   He made no delay, but rode on speedily.
   Those cruel villains soon made him their victim
   And put him to sleep without – hush-oh-bye baby.

6 My husband being scarcely a half a year buried
   When those cruel villains walked in on my floor,
   Demanding the rent before time was due, sir,
   And pay it I should or walk out in the door.
   I being after laying out all my money
   To bury my husband, it's plain to be seen;
   All I would say, sir, it all proved in vain, for
   They gave me the road to sing hush-oh-bye baby.'

7 I thought to proceed, but she made me no answer;
   Her tongue it became speechless and her eyes became dim.
   She let go the babe that she had in her arms,
   And down to the ground she instantly fell.
   'Twas quickly I ran and took her in my arms –
   'Cheer up, my good woman and come home with me.'
   All I can say, sir, it all proved in vain; for
   Her last dying words were: 'Hush-oh-bye baby.'

8 'Twas quickly I ran for the help of some neighbour
   And brought this poor woman to some other house;
   And there I prepared for her funeral charges
   And put her three babes in the care of a nurse.
   It was not worthwhile to go to such trouble,
   For they once had a nurse that was willing and free;
   The very next day they took part with their mother
   And went the same road without hush-oh-bye baby.

This is no doubt a song which originated in Ireland where, in the nineteenth century, evictions of poor tenant farmers unable to pay rent was extremely common. Very often, following an eviction by the local sheriff and his men, the cottage would be destroyed to prevent the family from returning, leaving them totally homeless.
   I learned this song from Mrs Kitty O'Shaughnessy in Kingman's Cove, Fermeuse, in 1974. Her father, William O'Donnell, had sung it to his children as a lullaby. A.B.

55 In Memoriam

Jim Payne (CAPAC)
St John's, 1983

It makes me ve-ry sad to hear a-bout the last min-utes of the O-cean Ran-ger; to hear of the sup-ply boat that was close to her and how it braved the dan-ger. I-mag-ine how those men must feel hav-ing come so close to sav-ing lives but still so far a-way — a bur-den they will car-ry with them, ne-ver shake un-til their dy-ing day.

2 These men were brave, the only witnesses to this terrible tragedy
  To save their brothers from the rig, we know they did all they could do in
    fierce and stormy seas.
  And now as we must all relive the terror of that night through their own eyes,
  Even though a year has passed us by, the night air is still broken by their cries.

3 So as ODECO collects the coin, eighty million bucks from Lloyd's of London,
  Refusing to acknowledge blame, suing others as though the damage could be
    undone –
  Only money matters to them, unconcerned for the families of eighty-four men
  This company, their crass uncaring must by decent people be condemned.

4 My heart goes out to families who must sit there and listen to testimony,
  No chance to get on with their lives, always reminded of how things used to
    be.
  When will their sufferings ever end? Will it be made easier by knowing all the
    facts?
  I think not, their wounds will heal by nothing short of bringing loved ones
    back.

5 We all know that can ne'er be done, may their humble souls now rest in
    peace,
  And may the sufferings of their families and loved ones finally altogether
    cease.
  May this enquiry soon be o'er, and may some justice come from dragging up
    the past.
  May the days when lives are sacrificed for corporate greed soon be gone at
    last.

The largest semi-submersible oil-rig in the world, the *Ocean Ranger*, like the *Titantic*, was thought to be unsinkable. During a storm in the early hours of 15 February 1982, the rig was sunk carrying eighty-four men with her. There were no survivors. It was the first oil-rig to go down in Newfoundland waters, though, as has been suggested by some, perhaps not the last. During the enquiry into the cause of the sinking, the suggestion that the supply boats did not try hard enough to save the men on board inspired political satirist and songwriter Jim Payne to compose these lines.
  ODECO, or the Ocean Drilling and Exploration Company, is the American company that owned the *Ocean Ranger*.

56 Jack the Sailor

John Hayman
Ramea, 1977

Jack the sail- or came on shore as free it is his
for- tune, for he had plen-ty of gold in
store last time he sailed the o- cean.
'I'll go up to my true love's door to see if she loves
me or no, say-ing: 'Nance, will you wed, say yes or
no,' say-ing: 'Nance, will you marry a sail- or?'

3 Nance looked up all with a frown – 'Do you think I'd marry you, o no not I,
I will get some man of an high renown, do you think I'd marry a sailor?'

4 Jack put his hands into his pocket, pulling out two handfuls of gold,
Saying: 'Nance will you wed say yes or no,' saying, 'Nance will you marry a
sailor?'

5 Nancy looked up all with a smile, the thought of the money in her heart did
go –
'For I've been joking all the while, be sure I'd marry a sailor!'

6 Jack put up a public line, plenty of gold and silver coin,
Leaving poor Nance with a fret and a frown the day she refused her sailor.

Mr Power adds the following verse:

If you were joking I been just, and it's only a question of you I asked,
So I see 'tis money that you love best and you'll not wed your sailor!

MERCER 184

57 The Jam on Gary's Rock

John (Jack) Lushman, Sr
Ramea, 1977

Moderate, free swing

Come all of you young shan-ty boys, come lis-ten to my song, hear my sad la-men--ta-tion, it won't de-lay you long; it's all a-bout six shan-ty boys, so proud and so brave, 'twas in a jam on Ga-ny's Rock where they met a wa-tery grave.

2 'Twas on a Sunday morning as you will quickly hear
   The logs were piled up mountains high and we could not keep them clear;
   Our foreman said: 'Turn out brave boys with hearts so brave and bold.
   We'll break that jam on Gary's Rock with our foreman young Monroe.'

3 Some of them were willing and some of them were not
   To work on jams on Sundays and they did not think they ought;
   'Til six of our Canadian boys did volunteer to go
   To break the jam on Gary's Rock with their foreman young Munroe.

4 They did not roll up many logs when they heard his young voice say:
   'I warn you boys be on your guard, this jam will soon give way.'
   Those words were scarcely spoken when the jam did break and go
   It carried away those six brave boys with their foreman young Munroe.

5 The rest of those bold shanty boys the sad news they did hear
   In search of their brave comrades to the river they did steer;
   Among their mangled bodies a-floating down the gulf (?)
   'Twas dead and bleeding on the bank was their foreman young Munroe.

6 They took him from his watery grave, brushed back his curly hair –
  There's one fair girl among them whose sad cries filled the air;
  There's one fair girl among them who came from Signal town
  Whose moans and cries would fill the skies, her true love had gone down.

7 Fair Clara being a noble girl, the river man's true friend
  Who with her widowed mother dear lived near the river's bend;
  The wages of her own true love the boys to her did pay
  While the shanty boys made up for her a generous purse next day.

8 We buried him in silence, 'twas on the first of May –
  In a grave there by the riverside there grew an 'emlock grey;
  Engraved upon that 'emlock that by the grave did grow
  Was the name and date and the sad fate of our foreman young Munroe.

9 Clara did not long survive, her heart broke with her grief –
  'Twas scarcely six months afterwards death came to her relief;
  And when her time at last had come and she was called to go
  Her last request was granted – to be laid by young Munroe.

This extremely popular song has been sung in lumber camps throughout the United States, Canada, and Newfoundland. It is a song that 'everybody' seems to know.
  Mr Power refers to the place mentioned in the sixth verse as Sydney town instead of Signal town.

Singer's key B; MERCER 138

58 Jerry Ryan

Cyril Keough
Plate Cove, 1977

Now all you young men who go chop-ping, please
lis-ten a-while to my rhyme, con-
-cern-ing the year I was work-ing with the
fore-man, well-known Jer-ry Ryan.

2 We first met this man on the journey
   Who promised us timber in store:
   'Go up to the camp boys, to open,
   And stay 'til the job it is o'er.'

3 We quickly agreed to his suggestion
   And joined him in old Bishop Falls;
   Being eager for work and employment so scarce,
   Not knowing the wages were small.

4 We boarded the truck at the depot,
   Our baggage went back in the rear;
   'Twas little we thought as we journeyed along
   Of the hardships you go through up there.

5 We passed by pine camps and still waters,
   For our laughing and joking the while;
   And Dan with a bound, he brought her around,
   Saying: 'Boys, we are up thirty miles.'

6 Next morning all armed with equipment,
   A bucksaw, an axe, and a rod;
   With forty-nine men to make wages up there,
   With only scrub spruce on a bog.

7 It is hard for a man to make money,
   When it is only scrub spruce to be found;
   And if you refuse a bad chance on a scale
   The word is you've got to go down.

8 Seventy cents a day charged for your bucksaw,
   And seventy cents a day for your board;
   And then there's a fee for the doctor,
   Comes out of one dollar and twenty a cord.

9 We found no complaint with this foreman,
   I think he is honest and square;
   But it fell to our lot, like cattle were bought,
   And yoked to a bucksaw up there.

10 And when you lay down on your pillow,
    No matter if you're asleep or awake;
    You will think of the times you spent with Jerry Ryan,
    On the borders of old Rocky Lake.

John Ashton, professor of folklore at Sir Wilfred Grenville College at Corner Brook, tells me that this song is reputed to have been composed by one Mr Butt from Fogo Island at a lumber camp in Bishop's Falls in the 1940s. It is a protest song about the harsh conditions endured by lumber camp workers. This camp was likely owned by the Anglo Newfoundland Development Company (AND).

   I recall Uncle Mose Harris, who spent several years as a cook in a lumber camp, once telling me how sometimes woodsmen would chop off a finger or two to try and get compensation because working conditions were so bad.

MERCER 122

59 Le Jeune Militaire

Emile Benoit
St John's, 1983

C'é-tait un jeun- e mil- i- tair- e. C'é-tait un jeun- e mil- i- tair- e. A- près a- -voir ser- vi sept ans lais-sait en- core son rég- i- -ment. A- près a- voir ser-vi sept ans lais-sait en- core son rég- i- ment.

2 Dans une aubèrge il est rentré
  Dans une aubèrge il est rentré
  Bouteille de vin il a demandé
  Madame l'hôtesse lui-z-a donné. >bis

3 Tout en buvant de ce bon vin
  Tout en buvant de ce bon vin
  Une chanson haute il a chanté
  Madame l'hôtesse se mit-z-à pleurer. >bis

4 'Qu'avez-vous donc madame l'hôtesse?
  Qu'avez-vous donc madame l'hôtesse?
  C'est-il la chanson que j'ai chanté
  Qui fait vos beaux yeux bleus pleurer?' >bis

5 'Oh oui, oh oui,' répondit-elle
  'Oh oui, oh oui,' répondit-elle
  'C'est la chanson de mon mari
  Et je crois bien que vous êtes lui.' >bis

6 'Qu'as-tu donc fait méchante femme?
  Qu'as-tu donc fait méchante femme?
  Je t'avais laissé avec une enfant
  Et te voilà, quatre maintenant!' >bis

7 'J'avais reçu des fausses lettres
J'avais reçu des fausses lettres
Que tu t'es mort et enterré
Et moi, je m'suis remariée.'   > bis

8 'Où est-il donc ton second homme?
Où est-il donc ton second homme?'
'Il est à labourer les champs
Pour gagner du pain aux enfants.'   > bis

9 'Où est-il donc mon petit Pierre?
Où est-il donc mon petit Pierre?'
'Il est en-bas dans les vallons
En train de regarder ses blancs moutons.'   > bis

10 Tiens! Voici les clefs de l'armoire
Tiens! Voici les clefs de l'armoire
Prends-y de l'or et de l'argent
Et va rejoindre ton régiment.'   > bis

Although Emile is regarded as a raconteur and an inspired fiddle player, he knows a lot of fine songs as well. Christina Smith taped this one at a dinner party given in his honour. It is a version of 'Brave Marin.'

60 Jim Harris

Pius Power, Jr
Southeast Bight, 1978

In nine-teen hun-dred and thir-ty four, the last day-light in May, Jim Har-ris in the Ro-nald P. from St. Ky-ran's sailed a-way; he sailed a-way in search of bait, 'til he came to Para-dise Sound, when to his great and sad mis-take the I-rene he ran down.

2 As she lay to her anchor her crew was filled with joy –
Not thinking any accident to them was drawing nigh;
'Til the *Ronald P.* she hove in sight, more joyful did they feel –
With her swelling sails and her washing rails taking eight knots from the reel.

3 She was like some frightened animal with the white foam across her face;
Neither sheet nor tack now did he slack while entering in this place.
The boats were anchored scattered and for him there was plenty of room,
But he kept too near the *Irene*'s head and he broke off her jib-boom.

4 It pierced the *Ronald*'s mainsail about three cloths from the lee –
The mainboom left her mainmast; what an awkward sight to see!
It gave those boys such a big surprise, what to do they did not know,
And without her skipper's orders they let the anchor go.

5 O Harris he jumped on the deck, threw down his cap and swore –
Saying: 'Such an utter tangle I was never in before;
I been in charge of schooners great and small and they brought me far and
    near,
Across the broad Atlantic where the storms do rage severe.'

6 O if this was a youngster, what would the people say?
For an accident can happen to the best man any day;
It's all right when the wheel goes up, 'til it turns for to come down –
And you all might make that same mistake as Jim Harris in Paradise Sound.

This song by Peter Leonard concerns an unfortunate mishap in which the famous Captain
James Harris was involved. Pius Power says the song was at one time a household item –
as common as saying Grace!

61 Jimmy Whelan

Kate Wilson
Placentia, 1977

Irregularly

One eve-ning as I ram-bled by the banks of a ri-ver,
view-ing those sun-beams as the eve-ning drew nigh, it was
on-ward I ram-bled I met a fair dam-sel, she was
weep-ing and wail-ing with ma-nys a sigh.

2 She was weeping for one that is now lying lowly,
   She was weeping for one that no mortal can save;
   The dark rolling waters rolls carelessly o'er him,
   And yonder it flows over young Jimmy's grave.

3 'O darling,' she cried, 'won't you come to my arms,
   Won't you come to my arms from your cold, silent grave –
   You promised you would meet me this evening, dear Jimmy,
   For to wander alone by the side of the stream.'

4 Then slowly there rose from the depths of the water
   A vision of sorrow as bright as the sun,
   And his robes were all crimson in bright light around him
   And to speak to his true love he then did began.

5 Saying: 'Why did you call me from the depths of the water?
   Back to this dark world – not long can I stay.
   To embrace you once more dear in my cold loving arms –
   To guard and protect you from a cold silent grave.

6 Hard was the struggle I had in dark waters
   When those waters closed o'er me upon every side;
   But thinking on you dear, I encountered it bravely,
   Hoping that some day you'd be my fond bride.'

7 She threw herself down on her knees there before him,
   A-sighing and sobbing her bosom did heave;
   Saying: 'Take me, oh take me along with you, dear Jimmy
   For to die by your side in your cold, silent grave.'

8 'Darling,' he said, 'you have asked me a favour
   That no mortal man on earth can decree,
   For death is a dagger that we must all pass under
   And wide is that gulf, love, between you and me.

9 Now one more embrace, love, and then I must leave you,
   One loving kiss, dear, and then we must part.'
   Cold was the arms that circled around her
   And cold was the bosom she pressed to her heart.

10 Then throwing herself down by the side of the river,
   A-sighing and sobbing her bosom did heave –
   Saying: 'My dearest Jimmy, my own Jimmy Whelan
   I will cry 'til I die by the side of your grave.'

11 She died there alone by the banks of the river
   To be with her dear Jimmy whom she loved so well –
   To meet him in Heaven, her own Jimmy Whelan,
   In that land of bright glory with him for to dwell.

According to Edith Fowke, in *The Penguin Book of Canadian Folk Songs*, 'Jimmy Whelan' or 'The Lost Jimmy Whelan' was inspired by the death of Jimmy Whelan (Phalen), a shantyboy who was killed on a tributary of the Ottawa River in the 1870s.
   Although we have used Mrs Kate's tune, the text is from the singing of Mrs Mary (Min) Caul of Arnold's Cove, since her version was more complete.

MERCER 139

62 John Barbour

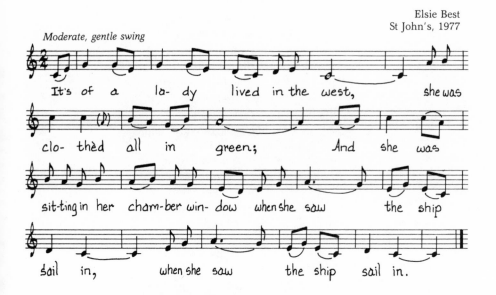

Elsie Best
St John's, 1977

Moderate, gentle swing

It's of a la- dy lived in the west, she was
clo- thèd all in green; And she was
sit-ting in her cham-ber win- dow when she saw the ship
sail in, when she saw the ship sail in.

2 'Oh have you got any bad sickness?'
Her father he did say;
'And the cause of your trouble I'd like to know,
Come tell to me I pray –
Come tell to me I pray.'

3 'No I haven't got any bad sickness,'
This lady she did say –
'But I am thinking of my own true love,
Who sails upon the sea –
Who sails upon the sea.'

4 'O is he a lord or a duke,' he said
'Or a man of note and fame?
Or is he one of our sailor lads?
Come tell to me his name –
Come tell to me his name.'

5 'He's not a lord or a duke,' she said
'Nor a man of note and fame;
But he is one of your seven sailor lads,
John Barbour is his name –
John Barbour is his name.'

6 'Now if John Barbour is his name,
It's hanged he'll surely be!'
'If you hang John Barbour, father,' she cried
'You'll get no good of me –
You'll get no good of me.'

7 Then he called out his servants all,
By one, by two, by three;
John Barbour was the first he called,
But the last came down was he –
And the last came down was he.

8 O he come down a-tripping down,
He was clothèd all in white;
His cheeks were like the roses red,
And his teeth like ivory bright –
And his teeth like ivory bright.

9 He paid them their wages with a smile,
And to John Barbour did say:
'If I was a woman as I am a man,
My bed-fellow you should be –
My bed-fellow you should be.

10 And will you marry my daughter Jane,
And take her by the hand?
And will you come and dine with me,
And go head over all my land –
And go head over all my land?'

11 'Yes, I will marry your daughter Jane,
And take her by the hand;
And I will come and dine with you,
But the heck with all your land –
But the heck with all your land.

12 For if you can give her one guinea,
To that I can give three;
Although they call me the young Barbour
That ploughs the raging sea –
That ploughs the raging sea.'

This song is known elsewhere as 'Willy o' Winsbury.' My Uncle Mack sings the same air and practically the same words, but calls the hero Young Willy. A.B.

Singer's key A♭; MERCER 196

63 Jolly Jack Tar

Linda Slade
St John's, 1977

Now as Jack was walk- ing Lon-don ci- ty he
met the squire and Nan- cy pret-ty; Jack
thought he heard lovely Nan-cy say the squire with her that night would lay.

Refrain:
Fol the dol diddle dair- o, right fol the dair- o- dee.

2 'I'll tie a string 'round my little finger
And I'll hang it out my bedroom window;
O you come there and pull the string
I'll come down and let you in.'

Refrain: Fol the dol diddle dair-o
Right fol the dair-o-dee

3 'O now,' says Jack, 'can I adventure
To pull that string from Nancy's window?'
Well, he went there and pulled the string
She come down and she let him in.

4 'What brought you here my naughty fellow,
To rob me of my gold and silver;'
'O now,' says Jack, 'come give me gold
I won't mention to any soul.'

5 Jack spent the night with lovely Nancy
And he tickled her right to her fancy;
He stayed with her all that long night
'Til it broke in the broad daylight.

6 Now when the squire came to remember
About that string from Nancy's window
Well, he went there to pull the string
But Jack was after pulling it in.

7 'Now since you've got above my garter
   No other man will follow after;
   I love you Jack as I love my life,
   I'll be your sweet charming wife.'

8 Now Jack got married to lovely Nancy
   And he dressed her up in silk so fancy;
   We wish them joy throughout their lives
   Jack and his sweet charming wife.

Linda Slade learned this wonderful song from the late Mack Masters, one of the foremost
singers in Placentia Bay. There are many Irish and English variants, one of which has been
recorded by the Sons of Erin as 'Yarmouth Town.'

MERCER 137

64 The *Kate* from Branch

Linda Slade
St John's, 1977

Ye feel- ing hear- ted mo- thers, I
hope ye will at- tend to those few
sim- ple ver- ses that I have late- ly
penned, con- cern- ing of the Kate from Branch that's
late- ly been run down, all by an Eng- lish
man- o'- war that's bound for St. John's town.

2 The man-o'-war that ran her down the *Royalist* was her name;
   Commanded by Captain Butler, to him we lay no blame.
   The man who held the morning watch 'twas he let out her light,
   I suppose to lose the boat and crew on that dark and stormy night.

3 It was on October the twenty-second as you may understand,
   The boat lay to an anchor about five miles from the land;
   As those poor boys lay on their beds taking their silent sleep,
   It was little they thought before daylight they'd slumber in the deep.

4 And less than two weeks after this boat and crew went down
   Michael Barry was sailing in the bay when young Daley he found;
   He brought him into St Mary's and he rode in a sail,
   If your heart was made of marble for that poor boy you'd feel.

5 Success to those St Mary's men, they are the real true blue.
   They bought him a shroud and coffin, now what more could they do;
   Likewise a boat to carry him off all on that very day,
   And have him waked among his friends and buried in the clay.

6 Being on the following evening they arrived at Salmonier,
   To see his agèd mother a-tearing at her hair;
   To see his agèd mother as she sat in her room,
   She cried and said: 'My darling son, you're cut down in your bloom.'

7 To see his agèd father he bitterly did cry,
   As the neighbours they all gathered 'round to welcome that poor boy.
   We waked him in his father's house all on that following night,
   And bore him to his grave next morn just at the clear daylight.

8 Now to conclude and finish, I have no more to say.
   Dry up your tears, offer up your prayers unto the Queen of May;
   Pray to the blessèd Virgin their sins for to set free,
   Unto the Lord, that Man himself, who died on Calvary.

This is a composite version of the song as sung by Linda Slade, who learned it from the late Mack Masters of Arnold's Cove, and Pius Power, who learned the song from Mr Billy, his grandfather.

65 The Leaving of Merasheen

Bride Rose
Placentia, 1975

At- ten- tion all good friends of mine, come lis-ten to my sad tale, con- cern- ing of an is- land down in Pla- cen- tia Bay; it was the home of child- hood times, my me-mo- ries still do stray to that lit- tle isle of Me- ra- sheen down in Pla- cen- tia Bay.

2 The people made their living on the land and on the sea –
They all helped one another, it was their policy;
With their little gardens by the house, and the boats moored to the pier,
With a sing-song in the evening, around a keg of beer.

3 Some time in December they turned out all the lights
And closed the doors of their happy homes they worked for all their lives;
'Twould break your heart to see them walk to the boat to go away,
So we bid farewell to Merasheen down in Placentia Bay.

4 No more we'll watch the caplin as they wash upon the sand,
The little fish they used for bait, to fertilize their land,
No more they'll watch their gardens grow or their meadows full of hay,
Or walk the roads in their working-clothes in the good old-fashioned way.

5 The houses now are all closed up, their windows no more will rise –
Their doors will never open again to welcome you inside;
Nor will you hear the sound of laughter, or the songs we used to sing,
Those days are gone forever now and so is Merasheen.

6 I hope you're settled down by now in your homes across the waves –
Although we're separated we'll meet again some day;
And from all of us who live far away and from our children,
We thank you for the happy homes we had in Merasheen.

This song was written by Mr Ernie Wilson while he was living in Nova Scotia in the late
1960s. Like 'The Blow below the Belt,' it concerns the Resettlement Program of the sixties
which moved families from the small communities and islands in the bays to larger centres
where it was supposed they would fare better; however, this was not always the case and
the effect on people was often emotionally devastating.

66 The Liverpool Pilot

Pius Power, Sr
Southeast Bight, 1979

O Li-ver-pool, Eng-land, is a place I love dear; I
spent all me mo-ney on whis-ky and beer. I
spent all me mo-ney- what could I do more? I was
forced to take ship and go sail for the shore. And it's
row, row, row, bul-lies, row, for the
Li-ver-pool Pi-lot she have us in tow.

115

2 It's early next morning we were out for a start –
We packed all our duds in the old baggage cart;
And straight to the landlord to get a last glass,
And on board of a ship us poor sailors was cast.

Chorus: And it's row, row, row bullies row
For the Liverpool Pilot she have us in tow.

3 One day as our ship she was calm on her line
Our captain was cursing 'cause he had no wine:
'Set tight sheets and halyards, let none of them slack
For they're flying aloft from her main topsail deck.'

4 Our mate and our bos'un all day going through –
Just looking for work for our sailors to do.
'Unreeve your jib halyards,' he loudly did roar –
It's 'Go aloft sailor, you son of a whore.'

5 Rounding Cape Heaney I'll never forget –
Each time I looks back and I thinks on it yet;
With the boats driving under and her sailors all wet,
And she ranged twelve an hour with her stern lines sot tight.

6 O now we are out and for home we do steer –
Our wives and our families and the ones we love dear.
Drink a health to our captain and pilot as well
But our old mate and bos'un, I wish them in Hell!

Mr Power describes this as a heave-up shanty that he learned from Doug Haynes of
Prowston.

67 Lonely Waterloo

Pius Power, Sr
Southeast Bight, 1978

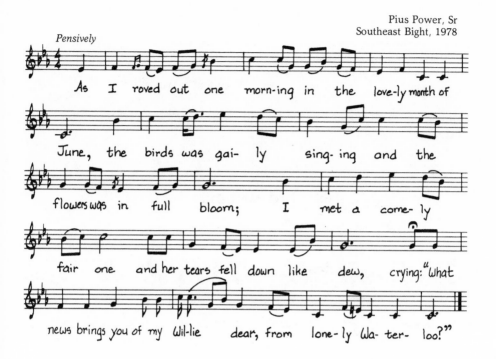

Pensively

As I roved out one morn-ing in the love-ly month of June, the birds was gai- ly sing-ing and the flowers was in full bloom; I met a come-ly fair one and her tears fell down like dew, crying: "What news brings you of my Wil-lie dear, from lone-ly Wa-ter-loo?"

2 'If your love was in battle could you tell me his name?
Dear madam, I'm a soldier and perhaps I knows the same;
His height and his complexion could you tell me it too,
And the colour of the clothes he wore in lonely Waterloo.'

3 'My Willie he was as clever a man as ever your eyes did spy,
He wore an highland bonnet, with a feather standing high;
A glistening sword hung by his side over his dark suit of blue,
That was the clothes my Willie wore in lonely Waterloo.'

4 'If that's the clothes your Willie wore, I know that young man well,
A bullet pierced his tender heart, from that your Willie fell.
He called me to his side and said: "Some Frenchman did me slew."
It was I that closed your Willie's eyes at lonely Waterloo.'

5 'Stand back, stand back young man,' she said, 'if what you tell be true;
You take me to my Willie dear, don't let me die with you.
The jaws of death might open wide and swallow me down too;
Since my Willie lies a mouldering corpse in lonely Waterloo.

6 O if I was an eagle, I'd fly those mountains high,
I'd fly to lonely Waterloo where my true love do lie;
I'd light upon his milk-white breast, pitch on his suit of blue,
I'd kiss my darling's pale cold cheeks in lonely Waterloo.

7 If I was but an angel, I'd fly those mountains high –
I'd fly to lonely Waterloo all where my love do lie;
'Tis for his kind and tender sake those bleeding wounds I'd heal,
And on his tender bosom forever I'd remain.'

8 When he found that she was loyal, when he found that she was true –
Put his hand in his coat pocket, saying: 'Here's the ring we broke in two;
I left you in your father's care and what more could I do?
I'm now at home, no more to roam from lonely Waterloo.'

Mr Power learned this song from George Follett of Clattice Harbour, Placentia Bay.

MERCER 147

68 Lord Bateman (A)

Kate Wilson
Placentia, 1977

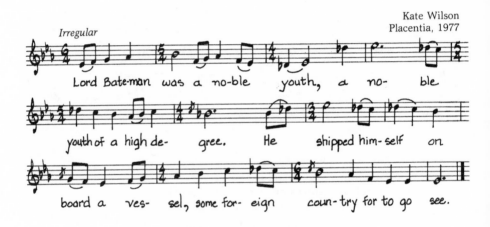

Lord Bate-man was a no-ble youth, a no- ble youth of a high de- gree. He shipped him-self on board a ves- sel, some for- eign coun-try for to go see.

Lord Bateman (B)

Moses Harris
Lethbridge, 1976

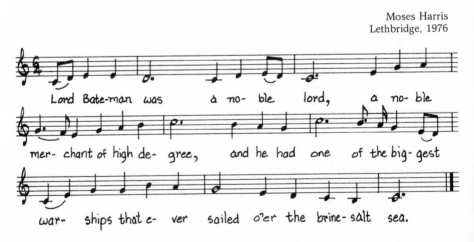

Lord Bate-man was a no- ble lord, a no- ble mer- chant of high de- gree, and he had one of the big- gest war- ships that e- ver sailed o'er the brine- salt sea.

2 He sailed east and he sailed west
   Until he came to well-known Turkey;
   Where he was taken and put in prison
   Until his life it was quite weary.

3 The proud Turk he had one only daughter,
   The only daughter of high degree –
   She stole the keys of her father's prison
   And vowed Lord Bateman she would set free.

4 'Have you got houses, have you got land,
   Or do Northumberland belong to thee –
   What would you give to a fair young lady
   If out of prison would set you free?'

5 'Yes, I got houses and I got land,
   And half Northumberland belongs to me;
   I'd give it all to a fair young lady
   If out of prison would set me free.'

6 She took him down to her father's cellar,
   And treated him with the best of wine –
   And every toast she would say unto him
   'I wish Lord Bateman that you was mine.'

7 She took him down to her father's harbour,
   And give him one of his ships of fame.
   And saying this: 'Fare ye well, Lord Bateman
   I'm afraid I'll never see you again.'

8 'Now seven years I'll make a vow,
   And seven more I will keep it strong –
   I won't wed with no other woman,
   If you don't wed with no other man.'

9 'Yes seven years I'll make a vow,
   And seven more I will keep it strong –
   If you don't wed with no other woman,
   I won't wed with no other man.'

10 Seven years being gone and past,
   And fourteen days being well-known to she;
   She packed up all of her gay clothing,
   And vowed Lord Bateman she would go see.

11 She went unto Lord Bateman's castle,
   And proudly she rang the bell.
   'O who is there,' cried the proud young porter
   'Now unto me your name pray tell.'

12 'O is this Lord Bateman's castle,
   Or is his lordship hisself within?'
   'O yes, o yes,' cried the proud young porter
   'He's now just taking his young bride in.'

13 'Go bid him send me a slice of bread,
   And a bottle of his best of wine –
   And not forget a fair young lady
   Who did release him when close confined.'

14 Away, away ran the proud young porter,
   Away, away, o away ran he –
   Until he came to Lord Bateman's chamber
   And he fell down on his bended knee.

15 'What news, what news my proud young porter
   What news, what news have you got for me?'
   'I just saw one of the prettiest creatures
   That ever yet my two eyes did see.

16 She bid you send her a slice of bread
   And a bottle of your best of wine;
   And not forget a fair young lady
   Who did release you when close confined.'

17 Lord Bateman arose all in a passion –
   He split the table in pieces three!
   'No more I'll reign in a foreign country
   Since young Sofia[1] have crossed the sea.'

18 Then up speaks the young bride's mother,
   Who was never known for to speak so free;
   'What are you going to do all with my daughter
   Since young Sofia have crossed the sea?'

19 'It's true I was making a bride of your daughter –
   She's none the better nor the worst for me;
   She rode to me on her horse and saddle
   She may go home in her coaches three!'

1 Uncle Mose pronounces Sofia as Sofier.

In *The Ballad Book*, William Allingham writes of 'Young Beichan': 'This very popular
ballad, of which there are numerous versions [including the modern one of 'Lord
Bateman'], seems founded on an adventure of Gilbert Becket, father of the famous
archbishop.' Though this idea has been disputed by some scholars and accepted by others,
there is little doubt that the ballad is of some antiquity.

Lord Bateman is indeed a popular old ballad which is sung throughout Great Britain,
Ireland, and North America. The two tunes given here are from the singing of Uncle Mose
Harris and Mrs Kate Wilson, but I have used only Uncle Mose's text since both are very
similar. Mrs Kate uses a different word here and there such as 'a slice of cake' for 'a slice
of bread' and 'he split his sword in splinters three' instead of 'he split the table in pieces
three.' Mrs Kate also includes the following verses not found in Uncle Mose's version:

She has gold rings upon every finger,
And on her middle one she wears three;
There's enough gold lace about her clothing
That would buy half of Northumberlee.

This verse would follow verse 15 of Uncle Mose's. The last verse of Mrs Kate's version is:

Lord Bateman fixed another wedding,
And with his heart so full of glee
Saying: 'I'll roam no more in no foreign country,
Since my Sofia have followed me!'

MERCER 148

120

69 Lovely Katie-o

Cyril Keough
Plate Cove, 1976

At twen-ty-one I first be-gun to court a come-ly maid; her fi-gure form it was hand-some, which had my heart be-trayed. I asked her if she'd mar-ry me or kind-ly let me know; it's for plea-sures I will wait a-while for lo-ve-ly Ka-tie-o.

2 She says: 'Young man be easy, and wait a little while,
Don't be so persevering, for I'm but yet a child;
For if you're inclined for to be mine, then away from you I will go,
And don't torment a virgin like lovely Katie-o.'

3 It was full of glee we parted when she said she'd marry me,
When another opportunity with she could not agree;
When a young man named Mike Whelan a-courting her did go,
With his coaxing and persuadence, he won my Katie-o.

4 Soon as he had her poor heart won, I'm sure he lost no time,
It was straight before a clergyman in wedlock they were joined;
Which leaves me here with a broken heart, in sorrow, grief, and woe,
And it's hard to find a girl like mine, sure I don't know where to go.

5 It would break the heart of any young man to see them passing by,
You could hear the charms up in Indian Arm as the bride and groom drew
    nigh;
With her crying out for vengeance, with her shouting to and fro,
And it's where to find a girl like mine, sure I don't know where to go.

6 Come all young men that go courting, a warning take by me,
   Don't never trust a fair pretty maid whoever she may be;
   Don't never trust a fair pretty maid wherever you may go,
   Like that one named lovely Katie, to me have proved untrue.

This tragi-comic song was composed by Mark Walker of Tickle Cove, Bonavista Bay. It seems that Mr Walker was courting one Katie, when Mike Whelan, a chap from Indian Arm (now called Summerville, Bonavista Bay), made off with the lovely maid. Mark Walker seems to have had his share of misfortunes with women – the scrap on 'Fanny's Harbour Bawn' is true testimony.

70 The *Maggie*

Moses Harris
Lethbridge, 1976

Moderate, with a swing

Ye fish-er-men who know so well the dan-gers of the deep, come lis-ten to a dread-ful tale and join your tears to weep, the loss of the schoo-ner Mag- gie and thir-teen pre-cious lives, which leaves so ma- ny homes be-reaved of hus-bands, sons, and wives.

2 At ten forenoon, November 5th, the *Maggie* sailed away,
   From happy homes near Brooklyn in Bonavista Bay.
   Light winds did waft her on her course, light-hearted was her crew;
   That Friday evening off the narrows the city came in view.

3 Our hopes runned high, our hearts feeled glad we soon should reach the shore;
   And turn to cash the fruits of toils upon the Labrador.
   The city lights they seemed to greet and welcome us to town,
   When Captain Blundon cried: 'My boys, there's a steamer bearing down.'

4 Straight unrelenting monster fierce she seeked her prey to get;
   She bore straight on us but we hoped her course would alter yet.
   We shouted loud in wild despair, at late an awful crash;
   Next moment o'er our shattered craft the angry waves did dash.

5 The scene that followed then, oh God, 'tis branded on my brain;
O rather would I join the drowned than witness it again.
When shrieks heart-rending pierced the air, a desperate fight for life;
A brother saw a brother drown, a husband saw a wife.

6 Of twenty-three who left their homes upon that fatal morn,
Thirteen of them are hushed in death and never can return.
The name of the steamer *Tiber* will fall in days to come,
On the ears of the Brooklyn people like the sound of a funeral drum.

The schooner *Maggie*, Captain Blundon in command, left Brooklyn, Bonavista Bay, on a passage to St John's in 1896. She was cut down in St John's narrows on 5 November by the *S.S. Tiber*. Thirteen out of twenty-three on board lost their lives.

MERCER 197

71 The Maid of Newfoundland

Carrie Brennan
Ship Cove, 1978

2 'Twas on the coast of Labrador I first saw that fair maid;
On 'Brador's cold and stormy shore, 'twas there my heart first strayed.
If I were rich or powerful, I soon would her demand –
For I could die without a sigh for the maid of Newfoundland.

3 I wish that I could speak her name, but prudence holds my tongue;
It's enough to know she's beautiful, she's charming, fair, and young.
Her breath exceeds the African breeze, that breeze by Zephyr's fanned –
O love is thine, I wish thou wert mine, sweet maid of Newfoundland.

4 The wild rose on its native tarn[1] spreads fragrance o'er the gale;
The modest bluebell sweetly smiles in many a silent glade.
I know a flower exceeds them all, I'll gain her if I can –
She's a maiden fair I do declare, and she dwells in Newfoundland.

5 Diana was a virgin fair, beauteous and comely, too
But not one word of sentiment or woman's worth she knew;
Her heart was cold she did disdain sweet Hymen's guiding hand –
O love is thine, I wish thou wert mine, sweet maid of Newfoundland.

6 I've seen the maids of different shades on many a foreign shore:
The French, the Greek, the Portuguee, likewise the swarthy Moor;
Chinee, Malay and Austrian maid, and the maids from Hindustan –
But for beauty rare none could compare to her of Newfoundland.

7 The primrose loves the sleeping green, the violet loves the shade;
The modest bluebell droops its head in many a silent glade –
I know a flower exceeds them all, I'll gain her if I can
She's a maiden fair I do declare, and she dwells in Newfoundland.

8 Prudence holds her name, I pray, assist you banns of love,
And I'll strive hard both night and day this fair one's heart to move.
If I should fail then come kind death and take your last demand –
From this world I'll part with a broken heart for the maid of Newfoundland.

1 Tarn is a small mountain lake. However, the singer could also be saying 'thorn,' which in many Newfoundland dialects would be pronounced 'tarn' where 't' or 'd' is substituted for 'th' and 'ar' for 'or.' She would be merely repeating what she had heard since she would never pronounce 'thorn' as 'tarn' but assigning the meaning of tarn to the word.

This lovely song seems to have been written sometime late in the last century by a Captain Duers or Jewers. It is not certain if he was actually a Newfoundlander or a foreign captain on a visit to Newfoundland. In any case, the man was certainly captivated by the beauty of a young lady who appears to have been a native of Carbonear. It is rather unfortunate that 'prudence held his tongue' or we would know the true identity of this exquisite creature.

MERCER 153

72 The Schooner *Marion Rogers*

Moses Harris
Lethbridge, 1976

Ye peo-ple all both great and small, please hear-ken un-to me while I'll re-late those lines to you that will loom in his-to-ry, for once a-gain it's in the news of a-no-ther tra-ge-dy, the schoo-ner Ma-ri-on Ro-gers was lost near Tri-ni-ty.

2 The schooner *Marion Rogers* she sailed from St John's town
Full laden with provisions to the North she was bound;
Seven good seamen formed her crew, so noble and so dear,
Of the most awful shipwreck, the worst one of the year.

3 But little did they ever think going down the shores that night
The hour of death and tragedy was on its silent flight;
The foaming seas rolled mountains high as on the ship did go,
The land it was invisible through heavy squalls of snow.

4 But those that's left to mourn for them, I hope will understand
That God is on the ocean as well as on the land;
And let our noble fishermen intercede with one record,
By knowing they're in heaven and have gained a great reward.

I was not able to unearth any information concerning this locally composed song, and
Uncle Mose could shed no light on it for me. It is rather fragmentary; no doubt more
verses exist.

Singer's key A♭

125

73 The Schooner *Mary Ann*

John Hayman
Ramea, 1977

You lands-men who all work on shore, how lit-tle do you know what we poor sea-men do en-dure when the stor-my winds do blow; St. Pat-rick's Day we sailed a-way in the schoo-ner Ma-ry Ann, leav-ing New York, our na-tive home, bound down to New-found-land.

2 The morning star lay on our beam as we slipped our lines that morn,
The monument stood in New York, we soon left it astern;
We spread our canvas to the wind to help our vessel on
Leaving New York, our native home, bound down to Newfoundland.

3 Our captain being a seaman bold scarce twenty years of age,
Got married to a loving wife six weeks before we leaved;
But little did she ever think as you may understand
That her husband she no more would see bound down to Newfoundland.

4 The second day we were at sea he in his cabin lay
And calling to his mate on deck those words I heard him say:
'I'm taken down in some disease as you may understand
To you my mate I'll leave full charge bound down to Newfoundland.

5 And if you makes an harbour on the Nova Scotia shore
Give me a decent burial and of you I'll ask no more;
And if we arrives safe in New York, my case you will make known,
I am dying sure,' he cried once more, 'far from my happy home.'

6 With aching hearts we spread our sails, his orders to obey
We made the land quite early, 'twas on that selfsame day;
And four o'clock that following day as you may understand
'Twas in Arichat[1] our captain died bound down to Newfoundland.

7 The doctors they were called on board our cases to make known –
Smallpox on board is raging and the truth to you I'll tell;
And four o'clock that following day four more were carried on shore
May the Lord have mercy on their poor souls, we'll never see them no more.

1 The singer pronounces this as Island Shott or Ireland Shott.

In other versions of the song, the monument referred to in the second verse is called the Statue of Liberty. This would mean the song was composed after 1886, the year the statue was erected.

In some collections, 'The Schooner *Mary Ann*' or 'Bound Down to Newfoundland' is assumed to be a native ballad, while in others it is considered to be American.

MERCER 103/342

74 Maurice Crotty (A)

Moses Harris
Lethbridge, 1977

Sit down, boys, and I'll sing youse a dit-ty 'bout the spring I was out in the Dan, Mau- rice Crot-ty being one of our num-ber, a co-mi- cal, queer fun-ny man.

2 He could sing songs and tell stories for h'ever
And lies he could spin by the score;
And when he would strike up a ditty,
All hands in her body would roar.

3 It was his first spring of seal hunting,
Not a rope on the ship did he know;
Not even to fold up a bunting,
Nor awkward to lace up a tow.

127

4 It was the daylight in the morning,
  All hands on the ice in a crowd;
  Maurice Crotty with his tow-rope and skin boots,
  Not a man on the ice looked so proud.

5 The ice we continued to copy
  I saw darling Maurice fall in,
  And I went for to save him from sinking
  For the water was up to his chin.

6 What course are you steering you blunder,
  You bobby, you dick-sided dude?
  'She's going all right now,' says Crotty,
  'Tomorrow she'll be in St Loup.'

7 Come port, come starboard, come steady,'
  She's gazing [sic] along at her ease;
  If we had a short-handled shovel,
  For someone to beat down the seas.

8 Coming home 'bout a mile from the steamer
  I saw Maurice stripped off for a bout,
  And big old dog-hood with his flippers
  Come straightening him out every clout.

9 'I challenged him there,' said poor Maurice,
  'For a fight if before me he'd stand;
  He took the mean dirty advantage
  And hit me with rocks in his hands.'

10 We backed him in turns to the steamer
  And tucked him up snugly in bed;
  Next morning he came to his senses
  And called me outside and then said:

11 'He must have got drunk from the liquor
  For that he could beat me to death;
  I'm certain he had a nice jag on,
  I got the smell of 'Old Tom' from his breath.'

Maurice Crotty (B)

Pius Power, Sr
Southeast Bight, 1978

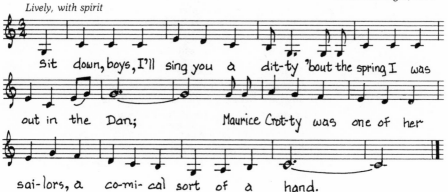

Lively, with spirit

Sit down, boys, I'll sing you a dit-ty 'bout the spring I was out in the Dan; Maurice Crot-ty was one of her sai-lors, a co-mi-cal sort of a hand.

2 He could spin off old yarns by the hour,
   And lies he would tell by the score;
   When Maurice would strike up a ditty,
   All hands in her body would roar.

3 It being his first year of seal hunting,
   Not a rope on the ship did he know;
   Not even to lace up a bunting
   And awkward to tie up a tow.

4 McCarthy hauled six, he was stronger
   And Mullins could only haul two;
   I'm sure that himself and Maurice Crotty
   Were the only slack men in the crew.

5 Now our captain cried out on one morning,
   'Come Crotty, your trick to the wheel';
   He shook like a bag of live kittens,
   And nervous and timid did feel.

6 'What course is she going?' said our captain,
   To Maurice who made this reply:
   'She's going all right, sir,' said Maurice,
   'Like a rat with a pain in her side.'

7 'What course is she going, you novice,
   You jackass, you dunderhead fool?'
   'She's going all right, sir,' said Maurice,
   'In the morning we'll send in good news.'

8 'She's on the Baccalieu,'[1] cries our captain,
   'Bedad I can't see, 'tis so dark;
   If she keeps on like this 'til morning
   We'll be in on a-back of the park.'

9 We struck the white coats the next morning,
And over her sides every man;
With his gaff, his skin boots, and his tow-line,
He's copying from (ice) pan to pan.

10 I saw Maurice 'bout a half-mile behind us,
He's cutting all kinds of queer frills;
He's stepping from tiptoe to tiptoe,
Like a farmer was setting out drills.

11 Coming home to the steamer that evening
See Maurice goin' off with the crowd,
With his gaff, his skin boots, and his tow-line
Not a man on our ship were more proud.

12 Coming home to the steamer one evening
Poor Maurice I saw him fall in,
I runned for to keep him from drowning
For the water was up to his chin.

13 We passed a big steamer's lights blazing,
Poor Maurice he whispered to me:
'O what a grand sight, Mr Daly
Apothecary's shop on the sea.'

14 'Does the swordfish go in for hop bitters?'
Said Maurice to me with a frown;
'Is there anyone laid up with the measels,
It's strange to see drugstores leave town.'

15 Coming home to the steamer next evening,
We saw Maurice stripped off in his blouse;
And big old dog-hood with his flippers,
And he laying him out every clout.

16 'I challenged him fair, sir,' said Maurice
'If fighting before me he'd stand;
But he got a dirty advantage
He had a big rock in each hand.'

17 I went for to see him next morning,
Poor Maurice lay still in the bed;
I ris' him to make those few whispers,
And this was the words he have said:

18 'He must a-got drunk by the liquor,
Or else he would beat me to death;
I knew he had got a good jag, sir,
I smelled the 'Old Tom' off his breath.'

1 Baccalieu is an island off Newfoundland.

'Maurice Crotty' or 'Spring of the Wadhams' appeared in Burke and Oliver's *The People's Songster*. It is difficult to say whether Johnny Burke actually wrote the song or not. At any rate, the text is incomplete when compared with the ones printed here – there is no mention of the fight with the old dog-hood or the apothecary shops in the 1900 publication. It appeared in the 1927 edition of Doyle's *Old-Time Songs and Poetry of Newfoundland* as

'The Spring Maurice Crotty Fought the Old Dog-Hood' with the following note: 'Amongst sealers this song was very popular years ago, and no doubt many will be glad to see it in print. Maurice Crotty was supposed to be a lad from St John's, and his first experience at the seal fishery will be read with amusement by the old time sealers.'

The Doyle version is very similar to this one.

MERCER 155

75 Maurice Hogan's Song

Maurice Hogan
St John's, 1977

I pon-dered on those days gone by as I wan-dered
all a-lone, in a lit-tle spot I love so
dear, in a place that I call home. The sun was slow-ly
sink-ing down be-side the hill-side green, my
thoughts went back to days gone by when I was sweet six-
[Chorus:]
-teen. O how I long for those bright days to
come a-gain once more, but come a-gain they
ne-ver will, for now I'm six-ty-four.

2 That's where I spent my childhood days among the rocks and rills,
   To the banks of a lovely riverside that flows down Flatrock hills;
   The children playing around your banks, they're just as fresh and green,
   O that's one place that never changed since I was sweet sixteen.

   Chorus: O how I long for those bright days to come again once more,
   But come again they never will for now I'm sixty-four.

3 'Twas in these dark depression days we had no rum or wine,
   With a gallon of molasses why we'd make a drop o' shine;
   And an old quadrille, your heart would thrill to the fiddle and 'cordeen,
   We never had an orchestra when I was sweet sixteen.

4 We danced all night 'til the broad daylight, we wore our old blue jeans,
   We never had no go-go girls, we had no T.V. screen;
   But a pleasant smile you'd see upon the face of each colleen,
   They never wore no make-up then when I was sweet sixteen.

5 But the young girls that you meet today, a different sight you'll see,
   You'll see them wearing mini-skirts a foot above their knee;
   And when they puts their make-up on they looks like Halloween,
   Their mothers never wore the like when I was sweet sixteen.

6 O how the times have changed since then when I was in my bloom,
   Men from this earth that gave them birth have walked upon the moon;
   But the moon still shines down Lover's Lane as it shone on Fiddler's Green,
   Some forty years or more gone by when I was sweet sixteen.

I first heard Maurice Hogan sing this song at the Good Entertainment Festival in 1977. I asked him if he would sing it for me and he very kindly made a trip from Flatrock into St John's for that purpose. It is one of his own compositions.

76 The *McClure*

Pius Power, Sr
Southeast Bight, 1977

At-ten-tion all ye sea-men brave that sail the
o- cean far, and hear of the clip- per schoo-
-ner be- long to George N. Barry.[1] With her
sails all set and she cast her lines and slow- ly
left the pier; in charge with Cap- tain
Tay- lor, who be- longed to Car- bo- near.

2 The *McClure* she left the thirteenth of March for Naples she was bound;
　She's a clipper of the sailing fleet with timbers strong and sound.
　She carried a load of fish in bulk, rough weather for to meet,
　Until she reached Gibraltar she was the beauty of the fleet.

3 A sharp look out for submarines, a watch by every eye,
　When Allen Barrett at her wheel a submarine did spy;
　He told the captain and the mate if what he saw proved true,
　Our captain he gave orders to heave the schooner to.

4 We lowered our canvas right away, we lowered our boats that day,
　We knew that our schooner would be sunk and soon would row away;
　The lieutenant and three of her sailors have rowed on board of our craft,
　He placed one bomb in her fo'castle and another he put aft.

5 They ordered us to leave the ship, so we done right away,
　Left to the mercy of the waves to row that livelong day;
　And what provisions we had on board and oilskins from our crew,
　Our captain's sheet and sections and coastal pilot, too.

133

6 We rowed the deep that livelong day 'til very late that night,
When a good Italian destroyer that quickly hove in sight;
'Twas by their captain's orders when us he did discern,
He ordered all our crew on board and slacked our boat astern.

7 They asked us our nationality as you may understand –
But we were British subjects belongs to Newfoundland.
They landed us in Cadiz [sic] where we were cared for well,
'Til we arrived at St John's town the sad tale there to tell.

8 Six men composed our schooner's crew, their names I did pen down:
There's Allen Barrett and Bert Noseworthy, belongs to St John's town;
There's Charlie Steven and William Bailey and Bert Wills was our mate,
Those hardy sons from Newfoundland belongs to Twillingate.

1 Barry is very often pronounced Bar in Newfoundland, as it is in this song.

Built at Tatamagouche, Nova Scotia, the *McClure* was owned by J.T. Moulton of Burgeo for the salt-fish trade. While sailing to a Mediterranean port with a cargo of six thousand quintals of fish, the *McClure* was sunk by a German submarine off the Spanish coast on 22 May 1917. Captain Augustus Taylor and his crew landed safely in their lifeboat at a port near Gibraltar.

There is some discrepancy as to the actual method the Germans used to sink the boat. The song, apparently composed by a member of the crew and therefore a first-hand account, has it that she was blown up by a bomb placed aft and another placed in her foc'sle. However, two published accounts state that she was either torpedoed or sunk by gun-fire.

77 Me Old Ragadoo

Pius Power, Sr
Southeast Bight, 1977

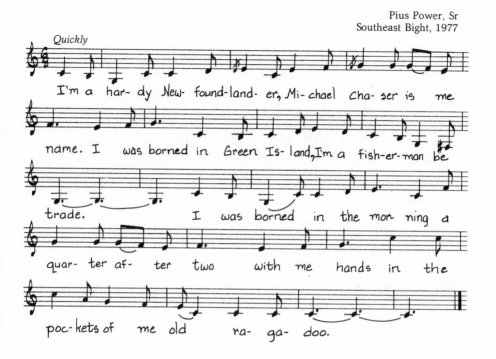

I'm a har- dy New- found- land- er, Mi- chael Cha- ser is me
name. I was borned in Green Is- land, I'm a fish- er- man be
trade. I was borned in the mor- ning a
quar- ter af- ter two with me hands in the
poc- kets of me old ra- ga- doo.

2 It was at the age of fourteen years a fisherman I became.
   I liked me job a-fishing and I wanted to be a man.
   I liked me job a-fishing, so a man I quickly grew
   With me hands in the pockets of me old ragadoo.

3 O I'm forty years of age and I'm not a bit ashamed,
   When I met a fair young damsel, Suzy Lagan was her name;
   And Suzy said she did love me, but I loved Susan, too
   With me hands in the pockets of me old ragadoo.

4 O I said my handsome Suzy: 'There is something I must say
   But still I think it cruel for to leave you anyway;
   To take you to the altar that is more than I can do,
   With me hands in the pockets of me old ragadoo.'

5 Oh up speaks me handsome Susan saying: 'I'm not put out about that
   For the time I knew was coming when you'd try to leave me flat;
   There's lots of men in Newfoundland that's just as good as you,
   With their hands in the pockets of their old ragadoo.'

6 O I buttoned up me overcoat, put on me old straw hat
   'Cause I really wasn't expectin' I'd get off as light as that.
   With the heel of me hand I wiped me nose and bid good-bye to Sue,
   With me hands in the pockets of me old ragadoo.

7 O now I am a married man and settled down for life,
In me cosy little corner with me lovely little wife.
But I oftentimes recalls to mind the time I courted Sue,
With me hands in the pockets of me old ragadoo.

Mr Power learned this song from 'old Steve Hynes of Southeast Bight about sixty years
ago.' A 'ragadoo' is a general name for a tattered garment, presumably with pockets.

78 The Merchants

Pius Power, Sr
Southeast Bight, 1977

I hope now that you'll pay at- ten-tion   and lis-ten a-

-while un- to   me,   'tis I   will re-   late a   few

ver-ses the truth un- to   you I'   ll   say.

2 It's all about the way that we're treated
It's cruel for me to express –
My heart it is filled with great sorrow
But really I will do my best.

3 It's all about the cruel rogues of merchants
No pity or love do they show,
They don't pity poor distressed cripples
Or widows or orphans also.

4 They don't pity us weary fellows
(That) are out on the ocean so grey,
In all sorts of storms and great dangers
Through toiling by night and by day.

5 When the black clouds is rising to wind'ard
And tells us the storm is at hand,
Those rogues they are at home on their pillows
Their darlings they have close to hand.

6 They'll kiss them, they'll squeeze those poor creatures
   And this to their wives they will say:
   'I have to have eggs for my breakfast
   New milk I will drink in my tea.'

7 It's then they'll prepare for their office
   Black figures and strokes they will make;
   'I'm now going to pay for my breakfast
   While the lads are out trawling at sea.'

8 O, now they are down in their office
   All luxury around them do shine,
   They don't pity poor distracted people
   They haven't got that in their mind.

9 When the gale it is rising to a tempest
   The thunder roars loudly on high,
   And the white caps do cover the water
   With rain pealing down from the sky.

10 It's then they will reef down their canvas
   Their dories they got to take in –
   The men that got poor leaky oilclothes
   They're dripping wet through to the skin.

11 When the ice it do cover all water
   And the mountains is covered in snow –
   When the poor rises up in the morning
   With the wolf standing close to the door.

12 His head it is aching with sorrow
   His bosom is swelling with grief –
   'Tis then he'll apply to the merchant
   To see if he'll grant him relief.

13 The answer you'll get is a poor one
   And this unto you they will say:
   'You better see some of your members
   Perhaps they'll relieve you today.'

14 Their hearts is as cold as an iceberg
   That freezes in the March wintertime,
   As the cold snow blows over the mountains
   By the strength of the north winter wind.

15 You'll think on the great sad disaster.
   'Twas the loss of the great *Florizel*,
   She brought rich and poor their last sentence
   And God only knows where they dwell.

16 There's widows and orphans to mourn
   There's hundreds was left in distress,
   But some they were got by good divers
   And some they were never got yet.

17 And also the great ship *Titanic*
'Twas built for all danger to brave,
But God found a way and they lost her –
She sleeps in a watery grave.

18 You think on the time that is coming
My dear friends, we'll all have to go,
To be buried out in the wide ocean
Or somewhere in clay, we don't know.

19 And when they are on their death pillow
With death standing close to their side,
Their friends they will gather around them
But still it won't keep them alive.

20 Great sums they will pay for their parting
A little more longer to stay,
You have to obey your last sentence
You're called and you must go today.

21 For you there's a place in the churchyard
The size of your coffin to lie,
Where you won't drive no horses or carriage
Or neither show up your great pride;

22 Your honour it will never save you
Or neither your bright shiny gold.
You pity distracted people
And don't let your heart grow so cold!

Mr Power learned this song from Mr Mickey Coombs of Fortune Bay while he was fishing in Clattice Harbour. The song was around in the 1930s and Mr Coombs said that old Mr Paddy Dover from Marystown had composed it.

MERCER 156

79 The Moonshine Informer

Moses Harris
Lethbridge, 1976

There's a qui-et lit-tle vil-lage in Bo-na-vist' Bay where the
peo-ple are u-ni-ted in e-ve-ry way. There is
one man a-mong them, I'll have you to know, he
proved an in-for-mer and his name is John Snow.

2 He informed on those people for making moonshine
And others for giving his wife ginger wine;
May his name be published wherever he go –
Buck goats and brave women torment you John Snow.

3 . . .
    . . .
He went down to Trinity his teeth to get plucked
He was seen and talked over by officer Tulk.

4 The authorities came over and they held the court –
John Snow with his clothes on dressed off like a sport;
With Polly for witness and Moody behind,
They'd swear that the water you drink 'twas moonshine.

4 He came out from the courthouse and this he did say,
'If tomorrow is fine I must go up the bay,
For to get my stuff don't you think it's all right.'
Not thinking those women would give him such fright.

5 Here's good luck to those women of Southern Bay
Likewise to Mr. Oldford who stands for fair play
    . . .
To banish informers down out of our bay.

Southern Bay is a small town in Bonavista Bay, close to Lethbridge where Uncle Mose
spent the last years of his life. At one time, he did reside in Southern Bay and was
acquainted enough with the local custom of moonshine making that he composed this song
in great condemnation of an unforgivable crime – moonshine informing! Apparently, when

John Snow went 'up the bay' to get his belongings, the women of the town chased him to the wharf and the man barely escaped with his life. It is most unfortunate that this verse has been lost.

Uncle Mose could not remember all the verses of this song; he found it easy to remember the songs he learned from other people, but tended to forget his own compositions – and he did compose a lot.

Singer's key A^b

80 Mr Costler

Margaret Carroll
Ramea, 1977

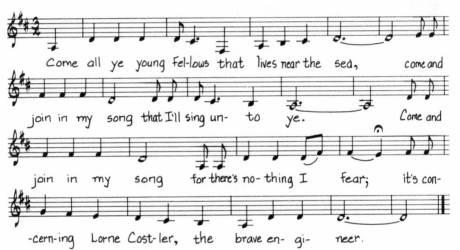

Come all ye young fel-lows that lives near the sea, come and join in my song that I'll sing un- to ye. Come and join in my song for there's no- thing I fear; it's con- -cern-ing Lorne Cost-ler, the brave en- gi- neer.

2 Now Mr Costler is a man you know well –
   He's well fixed with brains as many can tell;
   He has a large ship, *The Packet*, I'm sure,
   And you will not see the like for miles down the shore.

3 He was born in Red Island a long time ago –
   And he grew up from boyhood to manhood you know;
   And he started with a compass and likewise a map –
   You will never keep under a man in that hat.

4 He gained a prosition to carry the mail
   Around to those people who live far away.
   Fox Island and Coppett and all those poor souls
   Were given in charge of this mailman so bold.

5 Now I cannot mention in this little song
   Those wonderful things that our mailman have done;
   The way he has acted the things he have dared –
   So simply forget it and not put it here.

6 Only one or two verses and I must write it down
   About this coward mailman and how he came 'round –
   So now you can see it, it's plain my dear boys
   This is the worse service we had in our lives.

7 The day must be fine, the sea must be calm –
   Billy Warren get ready at Lorn Costler's command;
   'Get down to the engine and give her a prime
   Hurry up Billy Warren, we must go while it's fine.'

8 The skipper, of course, to the tiller will stand;
   He will look overhead and will view all the land.
   He'll rub up his forehead and wiggle and shake
   Like a dog with a rope that is tied to a stake.

9 Now you scarcely can see him he's so far away,
   But we know by the sound he's coming this way;
   His engine's still stopped but (by) his spyglass, I'm sure
   (He says:) 'What man in a dory is coming to shore.'

10 He gives out the mail at a terrible rate,
   Saying: 'The next time I'm coming I'm calling both ways.'
   (He) gets into his dory and goes down through the reach
   To jaw Billy Warren aboard the great skiff.

11 Of course it's too foolish for me to relate –
   I will never forget that particular day;
   Write it down in your log-book and keep it for sure.
   I can picture him now bearing out from the shore.

12 If I had more time I would make up some more
   About Billy Warren when he came to the shore;
   How him and Lorn quarrelled while reefing the sail
   The day they reached Ramea coming here with the mail.

13 Next day he reached Ramea on his homeward voyage –
   He took on board freight with the help of some boys.
   Billy Warren be ready and passengers too,
   Be sure and remember what I'm telling you.

14 Next morning quite early as you may understand
   He embarked in his *Packet* and came for this land;
   Jacky Dominy was one, the engineer he made two
   And the clergy for Burgeo this made up his crew.

15 How long he was coming I cannot relate,
   But when we did see him I guess it was eight;
   (He) got a cheque for the teacher and freight for the store
   And the next news we heard he was leaving the shore.

16 For ice there was none and of wind the same way,
   So you know it's the truth what I'm going to say –
   He's too big a coward and that is no doubt;
   We'll down the old villyan if he don't soon get out!

17 Now if that's not a humbug, there never was one –
   We'll write to St John's to see what can be done;
   We'll surely explain about this and about that
   For the old tyrant is now out with the *Norwegian Cap.*

18 So now my dear boys it's the end of my song,
   You can take it and sing it as you go along;
   Try and sing it aloud every day in the year,
   About this Lorn Costler and his brave engineer.

19 Here's a health to the captain and engineer, too
   But I hope you'll agree what I said about you –
   Write it down in your brains for I know they are thick;
   You can't come to Deer Island and get off your old tricks!

According to Margaret Carroll, this song concerning the incompetence of a certain mailman and his equally undependable engineer was composed by a teacher on Deer Island on the Southwest Coast. The islanders were obviously highly dissatisfied with their mail service.

I have assumed that the *Norwegian Cap* is a ship, but it could very well be a place name. It has been suggested that Costler could possibly be a regional pronunciation of Costello, a common Newfoundland family name.

81 Murphy in the Cupboard

Pius Power, Sr
Southeast Bight, 1980

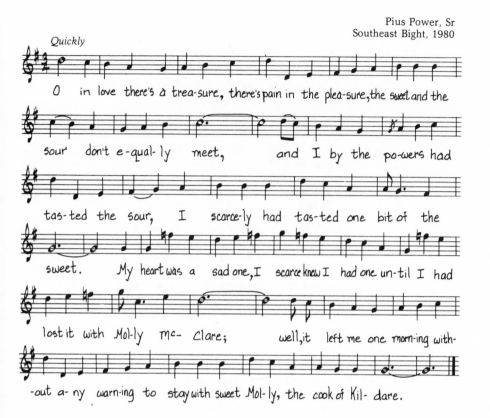

O in love there's a treasure, there's pain in the pleasure, the sweet and the sour don't equally meet, and I by the powers had tasted the sour, I scarcely had tasted one bit of the sweet. My heart was a sad one, I scarce knew I had one until I had lost it with Molly McClare; well, it left me one morning without any warning to stay with sweet Molly, the cook of Kildare.

2 The looks that sweet Molly gave, sharp as green holly,
   And it bothered me more than a mortal can bear;
   And I being such taken, in sleeping or waking –
   I'm all the time thinking of Molly McClare.
   She would not come near me not even to hear me,
   She shunned me the same as a mouse with a cat;
   She bothered my wishes and I got suspicious,
   My Molly had something I couldn't get at. ·

3 As I rovèd out on one clear winter's evening,
   'Twas Molly's own beautiful self I did spy;
   And just as I passed, sir, the door of her master
   I found it stood open and I slipped inside.
   The door it I entered and onward I ventured
   Right into the kitchen without being seen;
   With stumbling and poking, a-fumbling and groping,
   I found out a cupboard and shut myself in.

4 Soon Molly came thither, she had a man with her,
'Twas Murphy the weaver I knew by his voice;
Their talk was excusing and me she refusing –
Poor Murphy don't stand a great deal, a fit choice.
There was such a loud cracking and kissing and smacking
Possessed me with madness and envy outright;
And I being such taken and greatly mistaken,
Expecting Miss Molly some day for my wife.

5 I'd love to be viewing to see what they're doing,
To hunt for a hole might afford me some sight;
But knowing their appearance, I knew that my hearing
Would be just as good in the dark as the light.
A dainty fine posset I met in the closet,
And just like the filling my stomach I took [sic];
I knew it not sinful for eating a skinful,
Or tasting like Murphy the charms of the cook.

6 Soon Molly's sweet kisses got spoiled by her mistress
Who chanced to walk in, but no man did she see;
And Murphy for shelter set off helter-skelter
Right into the very same cupboard with me.
'Twas there he sat nigh me but still couldn't spy me,
'Twas nothing but darkness was there to be seen;
And when the old lady walked out I was ready,
I slipped from the closet, I locked Murphy in.

7 I candidly told him the closet should hold him
Until he'd relinquished my Molly for life.
The answer he made me: 'That's more than I can, sir,
Because it do happen that she is my wife.'
O since she have carried you slyly and married you –
O Molly, I will be revenged on your spark!
I'll serve him as you did me when you deluded me,
That is, I'll keep him shut up in the dark.

8 Just having the forecast of holding the door fast,
I put that poor lady in the hell of a fright.
She bid me unlock it, but into my pocket
I put the key safe and I bid her good-night.
'Twas soon I suspect that her master detected
This rogue of a Murphy and brought him on trial.
For stealing that posset I ate in the closet
He spent his sweet honeymoon locked up in jail!

This song was often sung or recited at Christmas or St Patrick's Day concerts in Clattice
Harbour and Merasheen. An elderly gentleman told me he once acted out the part of the
man in the cupboard, and everyone 'was in screeches' of laughter. A.B.

82 My Dear, I'm Bound for Canaday (A)

Pius Power, Sr
Southeast Bight, 1979

"My dear, I'm bound for Ca- na- day, and Sal-ly and
I must part, to leave be- hind a
blue-eyed girl with a sad and a bro- ken heart, to
face hard-heart- ed stran- gers all in some
for- eign land." The tears rolled down her
ro- sy cheeks as she took me by the hand.

My Dear, I'm Bound for Canaday (B)

Bill Foley
Tilting, 1980

Free time, slowly

"My dear, I'm bound for Ca-na-day, love Sal-ly, we must part; I'm going to leave my na-tive home all with a hea-vy heart to face cold-heart ed stran-gers all in a for-eign land." The tears come roll-ing down her cheeks as she took me by the hand.

2 Saying: 'Stay at home, dear Willie, you'll find employment here,
And do not leave your blue-eyed girl, likewise your parents dear;
Think how your mother's heart would break if you should go away,
And on your agèd father whose locks are turning grey.'

3 'Yes, I will think on them,' said he, 'on that you need not fear
For I will honour my parents, and love my Sally dear.
I'm here just now in St John's town no employment can I find –
I must away, I cannot stay, I have made up my mind.'

4 'If you do go,' said Sally, 'remember me each day,
It's for your health and prosperity for you I'll pray each day.
Think on the happy hours we spent as we rambled side by side,
And the promises that you made to me that I would be your bride.'

5 'The promises that I made to you it's by them I will stand,
For it is my intention to return to Newfoundland.
I don't intend for to remain on that Canadian shore –
How could I stay three years away from you I do adore?'

6 The steamboat now being ready for Canada to go –
He took his darling in his arms and kissed her o'er and o'er;
Her rosy cheeks, her mild blue eyes – those eyes did fill with tears,
She looked the perfect picture – her age was nineteen years.

7 So now this couple had to part, their meeting to an end,
He promised every mail that came a letter he would send;
He bid his charming girl adieu and fortune on him smiled –
Now every honest, decent lad don't leave your girl behind.

'Bound for Canaday' was collected by MacEdward Leach in Labrador in 1960. He says that the song was first popular in Newfoundland in the 1860s or 1870s.
    Only Mr Foley's text has been used, since his and Mr Power's were very similar.

MERCER 158

83 My Good-looking Man

Frankie Nash
Branch, 1976

Quickly

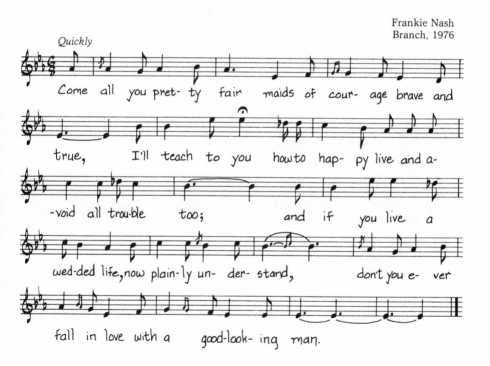

Come all you pret-ty fair maids of cour-age brave and true, I'll teach to you how to hap-py live and a-void all trou-ble too; and if you live a wed-ded life, now plain-ly un-der-stand, don't you e-ver fall in love with a good-look-ing man.

147

2 When I was sixteen years of age a damsel in my prime –
   I daily thought on wedded life, and how I'd be at the time;
   I daily thought on wedded life, it's pleasure I did scan
   I sighed and sobbed both day and night to get a nice young man.

3 My wish it seemed too soon I got one Sunday afternoon
   When home from church I gaily tripped, I met a fair gossoon;
   He looked so fine about the face, to win him I made a plan
   That very day I set my trap, for that good-looking man.

4 He said to me as on we walked: 'My dear and only love,
   If with me you'll consent to wed, I'll ever constant prove;
   I'll always be a husband kind and do the best I can.'
   My hand and heart I then did give to that good-looking man.

5 The night was fixed for us to wed, they bid us have all cheer.
   He gently pressed me to his breast saying: 'O my Mary dear';
   He gently pressed me to his breast and to the church we ran,
   And there I tied the dreadful knot with that good-looking man.

6 Scarce being a week when married, one Sunday afternoon –
   The day went by the night came on, off went our honeymoon.
   My gent walked out and so did I, to watch him was my plan
   When soon a flashy girl I saw with my good-looking man.

7 The kisses and toils and tales of love to her he then did tell –
   Thinks to myself now it's the time to serve him out right well;
   He did not me suspect at all so to my home I ran
   There sat down and waited for my good-looking man.

8 The clock was just striking ten when my gentleman walked in.
   I gently said: 'My Willie dear, where hast thou so long been?'
   'I've been to church, my love,' said he – O this I couldn't stand
   The rolling pin I did let fly at my good-looking man.

9 I blackened his eyes, I tore his hair, in ribbons I tore his clothes
   I then took up the poker and laid it across his nose;
   He just looked like a chimney-sweep as out the door he ran
   And never a lady loved again with my good-looking man.

10 Young married folks take my advice of high and low degree
   When a reckless husband you do get, pitch in to him like me;
   When I found out I was deceived, it was my only plan
   To disfigure the handsome countenance of my good-looking man.

Mr Frankie was very fond of singing humorous songs and he knew quite a few of them. As well as being a wonderful singer, he played the flute (which he called a fife) and tin whistle, and had quite a repertoire of tunes, stories, and songs.

MERCER 127/158

84 O'Reilly the Fisherman

Gerald Campbell
Branch, 1976

2 My love he was a fisherman, his age was scarce eighteen.
He was one of the finest young men that ever yet was seen.
He was proper, tall, and handsome, most beautiful and fair –
There's not one in this country with him I would compare.

3 John O'Reilly was my true love's name, reared near the town of Bray.
My mother took me by the hand those words to me did say:
'If you are fond of 'Reilly let him quit this country
Your father swears he'll take his life so shun his company.'

4 When Ellen got the money to O'Reilly she did go
Saying: 'This very night to take your life my father charged a gun.
Here is one thousand pound in gold my mother sent to you,
So sail away to Amerikay, and I will follow you.'

5 'Twas less than three months after while walking down the quay,
O'Reilly he came back again to take his love away.
The ship was wrecked, all hands were lost, her father grieved full sore,
Found 'Reilly in her arms and they drowned upon the shore.

6 He found a letter on her breast and it was wrote with blood
Saying: 'Cruel was my father who thought to shoot my love.
Let this be a warning, b'ys, to all fair maids so gay,
To never let the lad you love sail to Amerikay.'

'John Riley' or 'Riley to Americay,' 'Riley's Farewell,' and other titles, was very popular in England, Ireland, and America, and is well known through Newfoundland.

MERCER 195

85 The *Old Smite*

Linda Slade
St John's, 1983

With a gentle swing

Down in the bay last win-ter, I'm go-ing to ex--plain all a-board of a Yan-kee ves-sel; the Old Smite was her name. With our can-vas set and our an-chors weighed, all rea-dy for to go, with a load of fro-zen her-ring – she looked beau-ti-ful, you know.

2 While passing by St Peter's we had a lovely time –
   Up springs a hard southeaster, most seldom you will find;
   The wind veered off 'bout north-north-west, it blew a violent gale –
   Our skipper he gave orders to close reef every sail.

3 We tried her under a single reef but nothing would she do –
   And under a two-reef foresail we were forced to heave her to;
   And under a two-reef foresail our vessel she lay by –
   Our lives are on the ocean saying will we live or die.

4 For twenty-four long hours the hurricane did last –
   At two o'clock next evening the gale it came on fast;
   And on our noble vessel we quickly crowded sail –
   For twenty-four long hours we ran before the gale.

5 At eight o'clock next evening, our second watch that night –
The man up on the lookout said he had spied a light.
The captain he'd just gone below got ready to turn in;
Came up on deck, gave orders to haul her by the wind.

6 He then took out his sheet and chart and took our vessel out –
And by his careful reckoning (he told) how many miles we were out.
'It must have been some steamer's light you fellows saw just then –
We'll try her for another watch so swing her 'round again.'

7 Scarce had those words been spoken as we were passing by –
Our man up on the lookout cried: 'Breakers, ahoy!'
And that she will not clear them so every man stand by –
And on that reef or rugged rocks we ran her high and dry.

8 First when she struck those rugged rocks sure things looked rather blue –
To see our men like monkeys up ratlins they flew;
Two up in her main rigging, two more up in her for'ard,
And there they saved their precious lives by the mercy of our Lord.

On 21 January 1897, the *Yosemite*, Captain John McKinnon in command, was homeward bound to Gloucester from Placentia Bay when she struck a reef and ran ashore on Ram Island, about a mile and a half off the Nova Scotian coast. For a full account of this truly remarkable story, see *Dories and Dorymen* by Otto Kelland.

86 The *Penny Fair*

John (Jack) Lushman, Sr
Ramea, 1977

O come all you har-dy fish-er-men, and lis-ten to my song; now we're not ve-ry good scho-lars, and we won't de-lay you long. I have a lit-tle sto-ry a-bout the Pen-ny Fair, how she drif-ted from the wharf one night in De-cem-ber of this year.

2 Shake hands with Stanley Rossiter, boys, her skipper in command –
Shake hands with mate Abe Oxford, likewise his bos'un Ban;
They are three jolly fishermen as anyone can prove,
'Til they woke up this morning with the *Penny Fair* up in the cove.

3 Frank Andrews he did phone the men and he got them out that morn –
As they were tucked up in their beds so cozy and so warm;
George Dunford he leaped out of bed through the window he did stare
He said: 'Martha Jane, come and have a look, the *Penny Fair*'s over here!'

4 O Stan he hurried down the path to see the awful sight –
When he brought her open he knew she was all right;
He went out and spoke to Abe, said: 'I don't know what to do,
So I'm going over on the wharf and leave it up to you.'

5 O Abe he got out on the bridge and he began to shout:
'Come off and get the skipper boys, I'll try to get her out.'
He's going over on the wharf and going to blow the horn –
And when he gets the warps ashore, I'll give her a kick astern.

6 O Stan got over on the wharf and he spoke to Mr Reed
He tried to get the *Penny Wise* but Reed give him no heed;
It didn't look so very nice as it did blow and rain –
But ol' Abe he took her out of the cove and he tied her up again.

7 Jack Lushman aboard the ferry, he also went aground –
But he knew nothing about it because he sleeped so sound;
And Leslie Cutler called him out, he didn't know what to do,
He made a jump right out of the bunk and he made right for his shoes.

8 Jack hurried up and dressed himself and went upon the deck –
When he saw where they were at, sure he could hardly speak;
O Leslie Cutler had to laugh and Jack did laugh as well
'Cause how a man could sleep so sound no one will ever tell.

9 Now to conclude and finish, I know you'll all agree
In wishing success to the *Penny Fair* and the *Penny*'s company;
Likewise Captain Rossiter and all his gallant men
May they load her up where'er they go and bring her to port again.

This song was composed in 1970 by Blanche Pink, Ramea.

87 The Petty Harbour Bait Skiff

Moses Harris
Lethbridge, 1976

Ye peo-ple all both great and small, I hope you will at- tend to those few sim- ple ver- ses that I have late-ly penned. They are con- cern- ing dan- ger which our poor sea- men stand, while sail-ing on those stor-my waves by the shores of New- found- land.

2 This happened to be in the summertime in the lovely month of June,
When fields were green, fair to be seen, and valleys were in bloom;
When silent fountains do run clear that's sent by heaven's rain,
And the dewy showers they fall at night, to fertilize the plain.

3 We bid adieu unto our friends and those we held most dear,
Being bound for Petty Harbour in the springtime of the year;
The little birds as we sailed on sung o'er the hills and dales,
As Flora from her sporting groves sent forth a pleasant gale.

4 On Saturday we sailed away being in the evening late,
We were bound into Conception Bay all for a load of bait;
The sea-gulls flying in the air and pitching on the shore,
But little we thought 'twould be our lot to see our friends no more.

5 The weather being fine we lost no time until we were homeward bound,
The whales were sporting in the deep and swordfish swimming 'round;
Where Luna bright shone forth that night to calm amidst the sea,
And the stars shone bright to guide us right upon our rough pathway.

6 When we came 'round the North Head a rainbow did appear,
Every indication of a storm was drawing near;
Old Neptune riding on the waves to the wind'ard of us lay,
You'd think the ocean was on fire in Petty Harbour Bay.

7 We shook our reefs and trimmed our sails, across the Bay did stand;
The sun did rise all circlized with streams down o'er the land.
The clouds lay in the atmosphere for our destruction met,
As Boreas blew a heavy squall our boat was overset.

8 But Douglas Chafe that hero brave and champion on that day
He boldly launched his boat with speed and quickly put to sea;
He saved young Menchington from the wreck, by his undaunted skill,
His offers would be all in vain but for kind heaven's will.

9 When the sad news arrived next day to dear old St John's town,
There was crying and lamenting on the streets both up and down;
Crying and lamenting, crying for those they bore,
In the bottomless waves they found their graves whom they never shall see
no more.

10 Out of that fine young crew you know, there was one escaped being
drowned,
He was brought to Petty Harbour where good comfort there he found;
He's now on shore and safe once more with no cause to complain,
He fought old Neptune up and down whilst on the stormy main.

11 John French was our commander, Mick Sullivan second hand,
All of the rest were brave young men, belong to Newfoundland;
Six brave youths to tell the truth were buried in the sea,
But Menchington spared by Providence to live a longer day.

12 Your heart would ache all for their sake if you were standing by,
To see them drowning one by one, and no relief was nigh;
Struggling with the stormy waves all in their youth and bloom,
And at last they sank to rise no more, all on the eighth of June.

The Petty Harbour bait skiff was wrecked in 1852 near Petty Harbour. Out of her crew of
seven, only Menchington (pronounced Menchener by Uncle Mose) was saved.
   The song is attributed to the writing of John Grace, a St John's sailor who later died in
Brazil.

MERCER 167

154

88 Pretty Caroline

Moses Harris
Lethbridge, 1976

One morn-ing in the month of May as clear-ly showed the sun, down by some banks of dai-sies I spied a come-ly one; she did ap-pear as a god-dess fair, and her dark brown hair did shine, she ap-peared her na-ked bo-som there as pret-ty Ca-ro-line.

2 Her cheeks did blush like roses, all in the month of June,
Her eyes like diamonds in her head, her breath like sweet perfume;
The song she sung melodiously soon charmed the heart of mine,
As I stood listening to the merry deeds of pretty Caroline.

3 I said: 'My handsome fair maid, can you remember me?
I am a brave young sailor lad, that lately came from sea;
By loving of a fair pretty girl and her parents did combine,
They pressed me on board of a man-o'-war from pretty Caroline.'

4 But when those words was spoken, away from me she drew –
'Stand back, stand back young man,' she cried, 'or else you'll tell me true;
To produce a ring of brilliant gold, and a lock of hair is mine –
No mortal man will ever trepan young faithful Caroline.'

5 A ring of gold and a lock of hair this young man had to show –
He said: 'My dearest jewel, it's to some church we'll go.'
They got married in some mansion fair and splendid they do shine;
He blessed the day in the month of May when he meet young Caroline.

This was Aunt Carrie (Caroline) Brennan's favourite song. She said her husband would often sing it to her, and when she heard Uncle Mose perform it at the Good Entertainment Festival in 1977, she declared she hadn't heard anyone sing 'Pretty Caroline' in years. Uncle Mose made a tape of it for her.

89 Pretty Polly

Dorman Ralph
St John's, 1978

Quickly

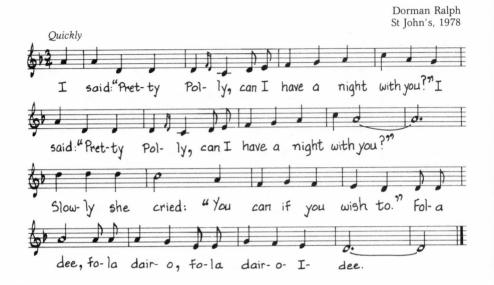

I said: "Pret-ty Pol-ly, can I have a night with you?" I
said: "Pret-ty Pol-ly, can I have a night with you?"
Slow-ly she cried: "You can if you wish to." Fol-a
dee, fo-la dair-o, fo-la dair-o-I-dee.

2 Well, she went up the stairs for to do up her beddie,
  She went up the stairs for to do up her beddie;
  Slowly she cried: 'Come on I am ready.'
  Fol-a dee, fol-a dair-o, fol-a dair-o-I-dee.

3 'Well, your room door is locked, love, and I cannot enter,
  Your room door is locked, love, and I cannot enter.'
  Slowly she cried: 'Come burst it asunder.'
  Fol-a dee, fol-a dair-o, fol-a dair-o-I-dee.

4 Well, he put his knee agin' it and he burst it asunder,
  He put his knee agin' it and he burst it asunder.
  And slowly she cried: 'Come in and lie under.'
  Fol-a dee, fol-a dair-o, fol-a dair-o-I-dee.

5 'Well, your breeches is tight, love, and I can't undo them,
  Your breeches is tight, love, and I can't undo them.'
  Slowly she cried: 'Take a knife and run through them.'
  Fol-a dee, fol-a dair-o, fol-a dair-o-I-dee.

6 'Well, I got no knife on me, sure that's a great wonder,
  I got no knife on me, sure that's a great wonder.'
  Slowly she cried: 'I have two on the window.'
  Fol-a dee, fol-a dair-o, fol-a dair-o-I-dee.

7 'Well, your lamp is gone out, love, and I cannot find them,
  Your lamp is gone out, love, and I cannot find them,'
  Slowly she cried: 'Jump in bed and don't mind it.'
  Fol-a dee, fol-a dair-o, fol-a dair-o-I-dee.

8 Well, they jumped into bed and 'twas tumble o jumble,
   They jumped into bed and 'twas tumble o jumble.
   Slowly she cried: ''. . .
   Fol-a dee, fol-a dair-o, fol-a dair-o-I-dee.

9 At six months being over pretty Polly fell a-weeping,
   At six months being over pretty Polly fell a-weeping –
   That's what she got by her snoring and sleeping.
   Fol-a dee, fol-a dair-o, fol-a dair-o-I-dee.

10 The ninth month being over pretty Polly fell asunder,
   The ninth month being over pretty Polly fell asunder –
   That's what she got by her night lying under.
   Fol-a dee, fol-a dair-o, fol-a dair-o-I-dee.

This song is a great favourite of Dorman who sang it with much gusto while accompanying himself, as he usually does, on the accordion. 'Pretty Polly' is also known in Newfoundland as 'The Young Doctor' with the following as the first verse of the song:

I am a young doctor and my price is one penny,
I am a young doctor and my price is one penny –
For curing young girls with a pain in their belly.
With me wack fol-a dol fol-a dair-ol-o-day!

157

90 The Prison of Newfoundland

Pius Power, Jr
Southeast Bight, 1983

Ye lads and lasses of Newfoundland, come listen to my sad tale, while I relate the hardships that I spent in St. John's jail. Although I'm a prisoner in this land, I'll do the best I can to relate the hardships I went through in the prison of Newfoundland.

2 On the twenty-first day of October to this country I first came,
   On a British brig from Baltimore, the *Poregram* by name;
   We were consigned to Harvey's wharf our cargo there to land,
   Which causes me bitterly to regret my first voyage to Newfoundland.

3 The day all of my trial it would grieve your heart full sore,
   When I thinks on Daniel Haggarty who falsely on me swore.
   Judge Carter passed my sentence and this to me did say:
   'Six months on hard bread and cold water in the penitentiary.'

4 O when my sentence it was passed then I was marched away,
   Down to the penitentiary my winter there to stay;
   Where I found comrades plentiful as you may understand,
   To live on hard bread and cold water in the prison of Newfoundland.

5 My prison was situated by the side of a lonely pond,
   Where oftentimes did I sit and sing like the mockingbird alone;
   Watching the lads and lasses how they used to sport and play,
   Through my iron-grated window in the penitentiary.

6 One night as I lay fast asleep in my lonely prison cell,
I dreamed I was back in old Ireland where once I used to dwell;
Those pleasant dreams disturbed my rest as you may understand,
'Twas there I awoke with a broken heart in the prison of Newfoundland.

7 Now to conclude and finish I mean to end my song,
Johnny O'Doyle it is my name and in old Ireland I belong;
I served my time in the Black Ball Line since ever I went to sea,
But now at last I am caught fast in the penitentiary.

8 I served my time in the Black Ball Line since ever I went to sea,
But very soon I'll be making tracks to the land of liberty.

Pius Power learned this song from his grandfather Billy 'Poer.' He made his first fishing
voyage to Merasheen aboard his father's schooner at the ripe old age of nine – he learned
this song during that voyage. It is often sung in unison at house parties by groups of young
men.
The Black Ball Line refers to a shipping firm's fleet of ships.

MERCER 169

91 The Quiet Village Tilting

Bill Foley
Tilting, 1980

Free time

In the quiet vil-lage Til-ting, where night sha-dows creep, through the
blue vault of hea-ven the stars gent- ly peep; And
fresh in my me- mory a fair one I see, and it's
oft in the twi- light she wan-dered with me.

2 I thought her my idol of no other dream,
But she was deceitful, sure I never deemed;
And why did they make her thus lavish her aid
And endow with such beauty this false, fickle maid.

3 I own she was pretty by boyish [*sic*] loved one.
   I thought her the fairest all others among,
   But beauty will wither no matter how fair
   And so I will warn you – young false one beware.

4 For beauty will wither as passes your days,
   And the up-coming flower will merit the praise;
   And perhaps you will suffer as you've caused me to do,
   And long for the love that was loyal and true.

5 Don't you think you have broken my heart wily dame
   Though plunged it is true in a tempest of pain.
   My bright hopes though shattered, they might yet revive,
   And kind fortune bring me a faithful young bride.

Mr Bill Foley told Pamela Morgan that this song had been written by a man named Foley about Agnes Sandy (Saunders), the belle of Tilting harbour.

92 The *Ravenal*

Isaac Harris
St John's, 1977

1 Come all ye fellow countrymen and listen to my tale
   About a well-known trawler her name the *Ravenal*;
   'Twas late in January, the weather being fair,
   She left her own dear native port, the Island of St Pierre.

2 Bound down on the Grand Banks and this their every prayer,
   To return again in ten days time to their wives and sweethearts dear;
   She left the Grand Banks early, she soon got under way,
   All hands being in a jolly mood, they were going home that day.

3 She being a steel and a sturdy boat, her crew they had no fear;
   The threatenings of a violent storm was showing in the air.
   The news was soon related and we were shocked to learn,
   [That] the boat due in at two o'clock, she had failed to return.

4 Then very soon a search was formed to search the ocean 'round,
   But no sign of the *Ravenal* or wreckage could be found;
   They searched for sight both day and night but nothing could be seen,
   From Fortune into Lories, from that to Lamaline.

5 Some wreckage now was sighted and the search resumed once more,
   Some of the *Ravenal*'s wreckage was found on Lorie's shore.
   She may have struck a sunker, but such things we'll never know;
   We only know her eighteen men died in the waters cold.

6 Never again will their footsteps tread upon their homes so dear;
   Never again will you see their faces upon the Island of St Pierre.
   But those that's left to mourn for them, I hope will understand
   That God is on the ocean as well as on the land.

The *Ravenal* was lost in 1963. The song was composed by Isaac Harris, son of Mr Moses Harris of Lethbridge, Bonavista Bay. He sings it to the air of 'The Schooner *Marion Rogers*' (song 72); thus the music is not repeated here.

93 The Red Rocks of Bell Isle

Pius Power, Sr
Southeast Bight, 1979

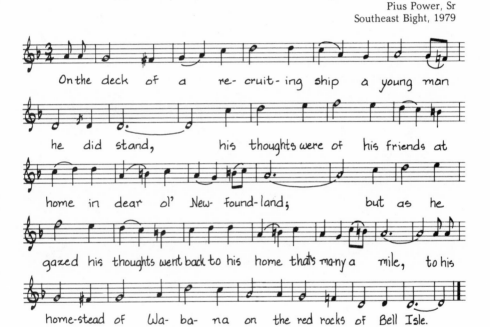

On the deck of a re-cruit-ing ship a young man he did stand, his thoughts were of his friends at home in dear ol' New-found-land; but as he gazed his thoughts went back to his home that's many a mile, to his home-stead of Wa-ba-na on the red rocks of Bell Isle.

2 He fancied he stood on the tramp going down to shovel ore,
   And loaded his twenty carriages as he oft-times done before.
   In the evening when his work was done he'd go home with a heavy sigh –
   He'd go and see his own sweetheart whom he thought would be his bride.

3 He dreamt he stood with her and gazed as the stars shone overhead –
   The moon it rose above the hill and it shone that night so red.
   It was little did he ever think of the danger over there –
   He was a Newfoundlander and I'm sure he knew no fear.

4 Then one night over on the front when a cry to arms did sound,
Among those gallant hero boys this Bell Island man was found;
He was wounded in the battle but he still kept fighting on –
The Germans were defeated and back home they had to run.

5 His comrades carried him back to camp and laid him down to die –
One man knelt down beside him with a tear all in his eye
Saying: 'Will you take this message back to my home that's many a mile,
To my homestead of Wabana on the red rocks of Bell Isle.

6 'Tell my mother not to weep for me, tell my sister not to grieve,
For I fought and struggled to the end and I fought it mighty brave.
Tell my mother not to weep for me or sigh with a drooping head,
For her son he was a soldier and among many, a gallant man.'

7 There's another not his sister in those happy days gone by –
You would know her on a gloomy night by the sparkle on her eye.
'You tell her I sent her all my love and to her I said good-bye;
Her true love was a soldier and for England he did die.'

8 'Now comrades I am dying, come ye say for me a prayer –
And before this battle it is won with you, you'll hear me cheer.
And when this battle it is won, I would like for you to sing;
It's down with Adolph Hitler, God save our gracious King!'

The mining operation referred to in the song was begun on Bell Island in 1895 by DOSCO Mining Company of Nova Scotia. Wabana, a Micmac Indian word meaning 'furthest east,' is the name the company gave the town because it was their most easterly mining operation at that time. The mine closed in 1966.

   The song refers to the Second World War, though it could have been written sometime after. It is similar in content to 'The Valley of Kilbride' and 'Bengin on the Rhine' – song moulds are commonly used in many ballad-making traditions.

94 The Wreck of the *Riseover*

Ernest Barter
Ramea, 1977

Come all ye hear-ty fish-er-men, come and heark-en un-to me, while
I re-late the hard-ships that do at-tend the sea; for
e-very year some homes are sad and we hear from day to day, some
fa-ther or some lov-ing son is quick-ly snatched a-way.

2 The *Riseover* she from Northern Bay with lumber did set sail
And she being deeply loaded and filled up to the rail;
For St John's she was bound my boys, her anchor we did weigh,
And with a sweet and a pleasant breeze the schooner sailed away.

3 We only being a few hours out when a heavy sea did rise.
In the evening it got bitterly cold with the blinding sleet and snow.
Towards the middle of the night a heavy sea did rise,
It was a hard and a trying time upon those sailor boys.

4 Our captain he gave orders that night to shorten sail,
All hoping that before daylight she would ride out the gale;
With a heavy strain she could not rise the sea broke over her rail,
At length the vessel foundered in the fury of the gale.

5 To save their lives a raft was made and it was quickly manned,
For every man was hoping that they might reach the land;
And as the raft got near the shore it quickly broke in two,
And carried away two fishermen of the *Riseover*'s crew.

6 The other two that reached the shore their hearts was filled with joy,
And turning quickly to sadness when they heard their comrades cry;
And as they watched them drive to sea as they stood on the shore,
They saw them wave their fond adieu 'til they were seen no more.

7 The *Fogota* she was put to sea to search the coast all 'round
But no sign of those missing men could anywheres be found;
John Pomeroy and poor Stradley they put up a terrible fight,
They lost their lives like heroes in the gale on Sunday night.

The *Riseover* was wrecked near Musgrave Harbour on 19 November 1911 with a cargo of lumber. Captain Pomeroy, or Pomroy, was in command.

MERCER 150

95 A Sailor Courted

Philip Foley
Tilting, 1980

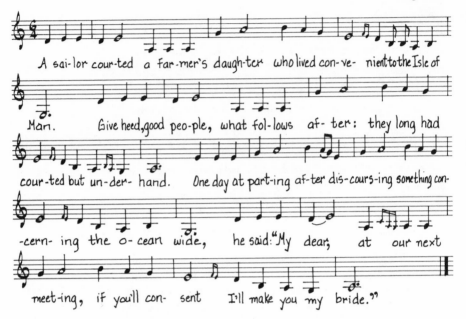

A sai-lor cour-ted a far-mer's daugh-ter who lived con-ve- nient to the Isle of Man. Give heed, good peo-ple, what fol-lows af- ter: they long had cour-ted but un-der- hand. One day at part-ing af-ter dis-cours-ing something con- -cern- ing the o- cean wide, he said: "My dear, at our next meet-ing, if you'll con- sent I'll make you my bride."

2 She said; 'For sailors we don't admire them
  Because they sail to so many parts,
  And the more they love us, the more they'll slight us
  And leave us after with broken hearts.'
  'You need not fear, my dearest dear,
  I don't intend for to treat you so.
  I have once more for to cross the ocean –
  You know my darling, that I must go.'

3 The news being carried unto his mother
  Before he put his foot on board,
  That he was courting a farmer's daughter
  One penny portion could not afford.
  One penny portion going to the ocean
  Like one distracted his mother ran;
  'If you don't forsake her, your bride not make her,
  I will disown you to be my son!'

4 'O Mother dear, you are in a passion
And I am sorry for what you said.
Don't you remember your first beginning
My father took you, a servant maid?
So don't dispraise her, I mean to raise her
Just like my father with you have done –
Therefore I'll take her my bride I'll make her
Though you'll disown me to be your son!'

5 When the lady fair heard the pleasing story
That she to sea with her love might go,
She said: 'My portion you need not mind it,
I might have money and no one know.'
'Money or not love, you are my lot love,
You've won my heart and affection still –
Therefore I'll take you, my bride I'll make you,
Let my scolding mother say what she will!'

When I first heard 'A Sailor Courted' I was immediately struck by the tune's remarkable similarity to an Irish Gaelic song 'Lá Fhéil' Pádraig' sung by Nicolas Tóibín on an old Gael-linn recording. The Irish air is much more embellished than Mr Foley's, but the basic melody is essentially the same.

96 Siúl a Ghrá

John Joe English
Branch, 1976

Like a spinning wheel

My love is gone to France to seek a for-tune in ad-vance;
when he comes back there'll be a chance.
Is go dtí a mo mhúir-nín, sláin-te. Siúl, siúl, siúl a gh-rá,
siúl go socair a-gus, siúl a dhrá. Is go dtí a
sa-ga rún. Is go dtí a mo mhúir-nín, sláin-te.

165

2 I'll dye my petticoat, dye it red
   Around the world I'll beg my bread,
   Until my parents wish me dead
   Is go dtí a mo mhúirnín, sláinte.

Chorus: Siúl, siúl, siúl a ghrá
        Siúl go socair agus siúl a dhrá
        Is go dtí a saga [*sic*] rún
        Is go dtí a mo mhúirnín, sláinte.

3 I'll sell my lock, I'll sell my reel
   When my flax is spun I'll sell my wheel,
   And buy for my love a sword and steel
   Is go dtí a mo mhúirnín, sláinte.

4 I'll go up on yonder hill
   There I'll sit and cry my fill,
   Every tear will turn a mill
   Is go dtí a mo mhúirnín, sláinte.

Following the Williamite Wars in Ireland and the signing of the Treaty of Limerick, the Irish army went to France in 1691 to serve under the French king. 'Siúl a ghrá' is the lament of a girl for her love who fled Ireland to seek his fortune in France.

Below I have given some attempt to indicate how the Gaelic is pronounced. Note that 'dtí' is pronounced more like 'dean' than 'dee.' This is due to the fact that in the dialect of Gaelic spoken in Waterford, from where many Irish Newfoundlanders originated, all final vowels were nasalized or had an 'n' added to them.

shule, shule, shule agraw
shule go soca(r)t agus shule a draw
is go dean a saga rune
is go dean a mavourneen, slanta.

In the above refrain, the girl is wishing her love farewell until she sees him again, and hoping he will be safe. Dying her petticoat red means that she is loyal to her love. The word lock in the song refers to loose fragments of wool or cotton twisted around the finger of a spinner at the distaff.

Skipper Dan

97 Skipper Dan

Moses Harris
Lethbridge, 1976

It's for the old Ti-ger, she's trimmed up a-gain, she's on the South-side with her bow bro-ken in, her can-vas tied up, and the men on the yard, and the cap-tain be-low with the mate play-ing cards. Lad-die

Refrain:

Fol-da did-dle lair-o Fol-lair-al-o-dee.

2 It was on a Sunday evening I went aft again,
   To borry some money from old Skipper Dan:
   'I'll give you no money for 'feard you'd get drunk,
   So you'd better go for'ard and turn into your bunk.'
   Laddie fol-da diddle lair-o, fol-lair-al-o-dee.

3 'I don't give a damn whether you gives it or not,
   For in my old clothes-bag some rags I have got;
   A pair of old shucks I've tied up to my bunk,
   And if rags can buy liquor this night I'll be drunk.'
   Laddie fol-da diddle lair-o, fol-lair-al-o-dee.

No doubt more verses do exist, but Uncle Mose could only remember the three printed here. Although we have tried to include the more complete variants of songs, sometimes all that remains is a fragment – in this case, the song is of local composition and not well known. These few verses, we hope, may assist the memory of someone who may have at one time known it. Mr Power recalls hearing men older than himself, or the 'old people,' singing it, and that the chap in the song who wanted to get drunk did succeed in a St John's public house called Strang's.
   There was a sealing ship called the *Tiger*, which came to Newfoundland in 1878 and was lost in the Gulf of St Lawrence on 19 March 1884. This could possibly be the same ship, since sealing ships tied up on the southside of the harbour where firms such as Job Brothers and Bowring's had their warehouses and processing plants. This song, then, would have been composed between 1878 and 1884.

The Loss of the *Snorre*

98 The Loss of the *Snorre*

Pius Power, Sr
Southeast Bight, 1976

A- round the coast of New-found-land, brave fish- er- men re-side, who spend much time up- on the sea, sub- sis-tence to pro- vide; but of- ten- times a gale swaps down, brings ha- voc to our shore, be-reaves our homes of loved ones, makes ma- ny hearts feel sore.

2 On the eighteenth of September at ten o'clock that night,
The elements of nature broke forth with fearful might;
Everything was in commotion by the bursting of the gale,
Which brought distress to many hearts and caused many a wail.

3 Many happy ones returned home back from the Labrador,
They prosecute the fisheries, oft-times have done before;
With loaded schooners full of fish the commerce of our land,
How glad we were to greet them and shake them by the hand.

4 But on this memorable night around Bonavista shore,
The destruction of the elements the like unknown before;
Here many a fine and sporting craft this time did meet its doom,
Some with their summer's catch on board lately arrived at home.

5 The fishing schooner *Harold F.* became a total wreck;
The *Olive Branch* and *Planet* too were smashed from keel to deck.
The foreign going *Reliance* to the waters edge cut down;
And many of our small fishing boats next morning were not found.

6 It was not on the sea alone but on the land as well,
The gale caused much destruction, it's hard for one to tell;
How many of our small fishing boats were smashed upon the shore,
And down went flakes and stages which caused a great uproar.

7 Out by the old familiar spot well known as Squarrey Head,
   Where foreign ships do anchor out by the old boatstead;
   To take the produce of our land unto some foreign shore,
   With skillful navigators and daring sailor men.

8 On Tuesday eve at three o'clock, a vessel hove in sight,
   Which proved to be a Norwegian sloop which anchored in our bight.
   The *Snorre* was the vessels name, she was chartered by J. Ryan;
   A brand new ship on her first trip to stay here for a time.

9 Ah! Little did these seamen think on reaching port that night,
   With happy hearts and merry jests, their spirits gay and light;
   Thinking of their beloved at home, those noble seamen brave,
   That soon two of their number would meet a watery grave.

10 On Wednesday night at ten o'clock the *Snorre* burst her chains;
   Through foaming seas was swept away in darkness and in rain.
   Rockets were fired into the air, a signal of distress;
   Their booming shots flashed o'er the sea, 'Help' that was their request.

11 A group of men stood on the bank they all seemed stricken dumb.
   They all stood up like statues, like men that had no tongues.
   Until out stepped Ford among the crowd and tears stood in his eyes;
   'My God,' he shouts, 'can nought be done to save those sailor boys.'

12 A rope he grasped into his hand followed by three more men,
   And rushed toward the stranded with shouts, 'We must save them.'
   Out, out into the raging sea those heroes quickly went,
   To save those drowning seamen, it was their whole intent.

13 A rope Littles threw across the wreck which the men held fast on shore;
   Until one by one they passed o'er it 'til the saved ones numbered four.
   But oh, alas, unfortunately two sank beneath the waves;
   Fate had its way and doomed those boys to meet a watery grave.

14 One of the two ill-fated lads was thirteen years of age,
   Who left his home in Norway on the *Snorre* did engage.
   Methinks I see the mother now as she bade her lad good-bye;
   As he took her hand on leaving home saying 'Mother don't you cry.'

15 The tears streamed down that mother's cheek as she held him by the hand,
   Saying, 'Now my boy be always true and do the best you can;
   May God protect you on this voyage, his blessings follow thee,
   And keep thee from all dangers that do attend the sea.'

16 The other lad was older and shipped as A & B,
   Who supported his aged parents by his earnings made at sea.
   Oh, little did these parents think as they bade the lad good-bye,
   How soon the news would reach them of the drowning of their boy.

17 All praise to Bonavista sons for saving these four men,
   To brothers Ford, Littles and Paul, all praise be given them.
   May this brave act go down for years, may it resounded be,
   How brothers Ford, Littles and Paul saved four lives from the sea.

The Norwegian schooner *Snorre* was wrecked on the shores of Bonavista on 19 September 1907. Two young Norwegian boys were drowned, and the four others on board were rescued through the bravery of J. Louis Little, Robert Brown, James C. Little, William Ford, and Eli Paul, all men of Bonavista; they afterwards received recognition from the Carnegie Hero Commission. 'A & B' in the song is an abbreviation for able-bodied seaman.

MERCER 178

99 Soup Supper in Clattice Harbour

Pius Power, Sr
Southeast Bight, 1983

Sprightly

On the eigh-teenth of No-vem-ber, as you all might re--mem-ber, the day being a fine one and fros-ty too, you know, and the eve-ning being ad--vanc-ing, they kept teas-ing me a-bout dan-cing; so to please their foo-lish fan-cy I did a-gree to go.

2 I knew I'd be accepted, but really not expected
It bein' so long since I had been to anything before.
To the party boldly ventured and the ballroom door I entered,
I addressed the porter gently as he stood inside the door.

3 Five cents was the admission and will be some addition
We'll add it all together, for the item it is small.
The old *Giant* was in the centre with the fire red and rantin',
And wood, you know, there's plenty, for those b'ys was never small.

4 When the b'ys they got out dancin', I'll bet they were not prancin'
For every b'y and girl there they did the best they could;
And some would make a blunder like a double clap of thunder
But no one seemed to wonder when the sport is going good.

172

5 I gazed around the buildin' like someone was bewildered,
When something caught my sight about a little way ahead;
I discovered there the altar where the Holy Mass was offered,
But tonight it's decorated with buns of daily bread.

6 Oh, the waiters they were seven, between ten and eleven,
And you bet that they were fussy when the table they did set –
Now the soup so fast was comin' there was b'ys with boilers runnin',
'Twould make you all feel funny at what you're goin' to get.

7 The table seated twenty and soup, you know, was plenty,
And bread and buns went with the eats to make it all go good.
But what it was made out of, it is no odds about it,
For no one seems to doubt it, and the taste it suited good.

8 When supper it was over, like a storm in the Streets of Dover,
The music never slackened, and the dancin' still held on;
The old women started dancin', 'twas in bunches they went prancin'
I thought they were goin' frantic, but we had a jolly time.

9 For anyone that stopped between four and five o'clock,
They had another supper, it was just as much, or more.
I'm sure it can't be eaten or neither will be beaten,
Indeed it won't be equalled, neither up nor down the shore.

'Soup Supper in Clattice Harbour' or 'The Buns of Daily Bread' was written by Peter
Leonard about a local 'Time' – probably the most popular form of socializing and
entertainment in rural Newfoundland until recent years. These 'Times' usually included a
'sale of works,' 'soup supper,' and a dance later in the evening. Children were always
allowed to stay and were bundled up in coats and put to sleep on the tables and desks in
the school or hall. Baby-sitting was a function of the community. Giant was the brand
name of an old wood and coal stove.

100 South Carolina State

Edward Ward
Southeast Bight, 1976

When I was young and in- no- cent I left my hap- py
home; to seek for sport and plea- sure, so far from
home did roam. I en- lis-ted to go in the nor- thern
wars to fight for gold so bright, but they served me
so se- vere- ly, I left them in the night.

2 Now I was overtaken and forced all for to stand;
They bound my feet with iron, they handcuffed my two hands.
They locked me in a dreadful cell to meet my coming doom,
And they sentenced me all for to die on the twenty-fourth of June.

3 Come all ye young and youthful friends, I know ye will draw near,
And listen unto those few lines, for me ye'll shed a tear;
I'm here in close confinement to meet my coming fate,
And so far from home, I'm here alone in South Carolina State.

4 'Tis God help my old father, for when he reads those lines,
Likewise my tender mother, what comfort will she find?
Likewise my young and youthful friends, for me ye'll heave a sigh;
When I thinks on my happy home 'tis hard for me to die.

5 Here's adieu unto my brother, his face no more I'll see,
Likewise my loving sister that was so fond of me;
Tomorrow at nine I'm going to die all by my comrades' hands,
And so far from home I'm here alone in this a distant land.

6 There's one thing more I'll ask of ye, to send my body home,
And bury it with my sister beneath the marble stone,
And plant upon my gay young breast that weeping willow tree,
Where many's the young and youthful friend will shed a tear for me.

According to Edward Ward, this song is about a Newfoundlander who went to fight in
the war for American independence. The air is quite unusual, and beautifully sad.

101 The *Southern Cross*

Carrie Brennan
Ship Cove, 1978

With a quiet grace

Gai- ly flags were proud-ly wav- ing at the
hour she set For brav-ing, all the ob- sta-
-cles ad- vanc- ing on that fro- zen field of ice;
and her crew no dan- ger fear- ing, proud-ly caught the
strength of cheer-ing; on the morn-ing of her
sail- ing, ma- ny hearts they did re- joice.

2 Our feelings we expressed them, when we knew that God had left them,
When we heard that they were sighted deeply laden on the foam;
And our hearts were glad and cheery when told near old Cape St Mary's –
By the *Portia* she was sighted and she proudly sailing home.

3 Sadly now our hearts are mourning, dreaming yet of her returning,
Many more with sorrow laden say the ocean is her doom;
O ye waters merrily prancing, with the sunshine on you dancing,
O swift us back a message, just to lift this veil of gloom.

4 Where is she you breezes, won't you whisper grief or cheer us –
Come if you please and let us know what has become of them,
Who left sisters and fond brothers, tender-hearted wives and mothers;
O swift us back a message, tell us what has become of them.

5 Tell us is she sank or stranded, was she swallowed or abandoned –
Are the waves that rolled upon them a forlorn and helpless wreck;
O ye breezes won't ye tell us where are the noble fellows,
We cheered the day they left us, crowding joyously on her deck.

6 Many hearts are sorrow laden, there's the matron and the maiden,
  And the darling orphan children may God hear their helpless cry –
  O look down on them each morrow, give them strength to bear their sorrow,
  It is you dear Lord can do it from your mansion in the sky.

The *Southern Cross* was lost in the spring of 1914 when returning to St John's from the ice. She was full laden with seal pelts and was last sighted by the *Portia*. Between 170 and 173 men lost their lives, and there was never a trace found of the ship or crew. This was a particularly sad and tragic time for Newfoundland since the crew of the sealing ship *Newfoundland* were lost on the ice in the same storm, leaving a total of about 252 dead in one month. There is another more well-known song written about the same event but I believe this is the first time this song has appeared in print.

102 The Spanish Captain

Elsie Best
St John's, 1976

Ye mu-ses nine, let you com-bine and lis-ten to my song; 'tis a mourn-ful la-men-ta-tion, it won't de-lay you long. It's of a Spa-nish cap-tain, as you may un-der-stand, he left his home in sun-ny Spain, bound down to New-found-land.

2 His wife she stepped on board with him dressed up in silk so fine.
  Her eyes was of the sparkling bright like diamonds they did shine.
  Her skin just like the snow blossom that falls before the rain.
  Her hair hung down in ringlets, Rosanna was her name.

176

3 Their daughter followed after them just like some angel bright –
  She had a small and a slender waist dressed up in muslin white;
  All red and rosy was her cheeks, from Spanish Town she came –
  She's fairer than Rosanna, who's called the flower of Spain.

4 On the twentieth day of last July, from home we did set sail –
  With the *Helen* in our company, blew a sweet and a pleasant gale;
  With the *Helen* in our company, we could no longer stay,
  For she got in that very night when we were cast away.

5 The Farmers and the Virgin Banks they boldly made a stand,
  With burning bait upon the ground to purify the land;
  The smoke lay flying o'er the hills and pitching on the sea –
  Our ship arrived no more across, for this was our last day.

6 The *Margrietta* was our ship's name, she was a handsome boat –
  With lofty yards and pitch pine spars she was scarce nine years afloat;
  By our reckoning and good conduct a due course we did steer,
  And our bos'un cried: 'There's land ahead, I'm sure it is Cape Spear'.

7 We reefed our mains, braced up our yards, and hauled her by the wind,
  But to our sad misfortune, [there was] no tug to take her in;
  For she had gone on business, she went the day before,
  With freight to Burin Harbour, around the western shore.

8 We squared away across the bay, that dark and stormy night –
  All hands was to their station, but no man saw the light;
  Says the captain to the bos'un: 'We'll heave the lead to sound.'
  No star nor moon was to be seen, nor pilot to be found.

9 The night was thick with heavy smoke, the seas ran mountains high –
  It was on that point, that barren rock we ran her high and dry;
  On the eighteenth day of August, o what a dreadful sight!
  All hands was in the water about twelve o'clock that night.

10 The captain, wife and daughter no longer could remain
  To enjoy the wealth and honour they left after them in Spain;
  For as they lay on their virgin beds the Trumpeter did sound,
  Calling [them] to the Seat of Justice where every stain was found.

11 Our captain being a Spaniard, a man of note and fame –
  He was a bold undaunted that ploughed the raging main;
  And I hope the King of Glory will his precious soul receive,
  And make his bed in heaven, where St Peter holds the key.

The *Margrietta* referred to is very likely the *Mayaquezanna*, a Spanish brig lost at Blackhead, near Cape Spear, on 14 August 1876. Both the captain and his wife were drowned.
  'The Spanish Captain' has always been one of my favourite songs to sing. It is typical of the heave-it-out-of-ya' type of singing so favoured by many Placentia Bay singers. The images in the fifth verse are quite arresting, albeit somewhat mystifying.
  My mother learned this song from her grandparents in Tack's Beach, Placentia Bay. A.B.

MERCER 180

103 The *Susan*

Pius Power, Sr
Southeast Bight, 1977

Ye dar-ing sons of New-found-land, come lis-ten un- to
me, 'tis I'll re- late that sad, sad news that
we re- cord to- day, the loss of four fine
fish-er- men, their friends will see no more, who
lost their lives at Cut-throat on the rug-ged La- bra- dor.

2 The schooner left in early spring the fishery to pursue,
Supplied with boats and fishing gear manned by a hearty crew;
Her friends they bid a fond adieu as they sailed out that day,
From their homes in Bonaventure at the head of Trinity Bay.

3 The schooner named the *Susan* with her crew from Newfoundland,
Sailed out of Bonaventure, Captain Miller in command;
And at her destination she arrived both strong and sound,
And soon her boats they did prepare to try the fishing ground.

4 O when the voyage they did complete and straight for home did sail,
The schooner met disasters in the heavy north east gale;
The heavy seas rolled down on her, rolled over hull and deck,
Those four brave youths from Trinity Bay they went down in the wreck.

5 'Twas soon the news flashed over the wire to say she was no more,
To say the *Susan* foundered on the rugged Labrador;
The saddest news of all do come that fills hearts with dismay,
The loss of four fine fishermen belong to Trinity Bay.

6 Most every year the same sad news from fishermen we hear,
To fill their homes with mourning for the ones they did love dear;
May God their sorrow now make light those loved ones left to weep,
For those brave hearty fishermen is buried in the deep.

Mr Power learned the song from his father when he was a child.

MERCER 150

104 The Sweet Town of Anthony

Edward Ward
Southeast Bight, 1976

Moderate

In the sweet town of Antho-ny, as I passed it by, in a neat lit-tle cot-tage I chanced for to spy, where the wa-ter runs clear-ly and e-very-thing nice — makes me think on old E-rin in sweet Pa-ra-dise.

2 I mounted on horseback nine miles I did ride
'Til I came to a cottage near the side of a road;
I said to myself, 'In some strange country,
Perhaps there's some bonny lass and she may fancy me.'

3 I 'lighted from horseback, went in and sot down –
This beautiful damsel I viewed her all 'round;
Her cheeks blushed like roses and her lips a pale red
And her eyes shone like diamonds as they rolled in her head.

4 I says, 'My pretty fair one, will you come along with me?
We'll both ride to New Ross and married we'll be;
Your friends and relations they won't on us frown
For to live at Blackwater near fair London town.'

5 'Young man,' she made answer, and this she did say –
' 'Til there's further acquaintance between you and me,
You know it's heart-aching and a trouble on my mind
For to live at Blackwater, leave my true love behind.'

6 New Ross is a bonny place, I heard people say
Where the small birds do whistle and the nightingale play;
Where the small birds do whistle and the nightingale sing –
I will sing my love's praises and then go away.

Edward learned this song from his father when he was very young. It is found in Irish folksong collections as 'The Sweet County Antrim.' Helen Creighton collected a version in

179

Nova Scotia with the name 'By *Kells Waters*'; in that particular version of the song,
Anthony is Antrim, New Ross is Bally Bay, and Blackwater is Kells Waters.
Anthony is pronounced 'Antny.'

105 Taking Gear in the Night

Jerry Fudge
McCallum, 1977

Moderate, with a swing

Come all my good peo-ple, come lis-ten you might, it's
on-ly a dit-ty I'm go-ing to write. It's
on-ly a dit-ty, I'm sure it's all right, it's
all a-bout tak-ing your gear in the night.

2 John Keeping come up here to give a first call,
   And with a loud shout those words he did bawl;
   'Get out jolly boys, it's a beautiful night,
   All hands are bound out taking gear in the night.'

3 For the first tick of the engine I think 'twas a-slick,
   Went pushing out through with a mightiful tick;
   With a moon up above and the stars shining bright,
   And hands are bound out taking gear in the night.

4 Old Sam said to Hughie, 'It's a beautiful night,'
   And damn it said Hughie, 'No doubt it's all right';
   They put on their oilskins at one in the night,
   Those boys were bound out taking gear in the night.

5 Well, the next man I'll mention it is little Toss,
   He left about three o'clock to go across;
   When the wind from the southeast it came on to blow,
   And back to the Island little Toss he did go.

6 You talk how your soldiers the battle did fight,
   The same of your sailors who did all their might;
   I'll put it in print, you can say what you like,
   Cheerio to the man who takes gear in the night.

7 They work on the sea a living to earn,
   And not for a squall those boys will not turn;
   They'll venture their lives their families to keep,
   When the stormy winds blow, and the billows do leap.

8 Jerry Fudge is my name, and it's I made this song,
   I'll sing it to you friends, I won't keep you long;
   I'll sing it to you, it's the best I can do,
   There's nobody knows what hardships they go through.

9 I have a-been fishing, I know what it's like,
   But never did I take my gear in the night;
   But now I'm not fishing, I'm keeping the light,
   Cheerio to the man who takes gear in the night.

10 Come all you young ladies I'll have you to know,
   Don't never despise a fisherman bold;
   But huddle and cuddle fond lover's delight,
   He'll tell you about taking gear in the night.

11 And now to conclude and to finish my song,
   The boys from Penguin Islands they soon will be gone;
   They're going to spend Christmas to lover's delight,
   And that won't be out taking gear in the night.

12 Now fishing's all over so late in the Fall,
   And the boys are bound homeward to drink their alcohol;
   And as they were leaving I heard them all say,
   Good-bye to old Penguin Islands while we are away.

I recorded this song from the composer, Mr Jerry Fudge, of McCallum, Southwest Coast.
He wrote the song during his time as lightkeeper on the Penguin Islands where he spent
many years. It describes the hardships that fishermen endure while risking their lives to
earn a living from the sea. 'Taking Gear in the Night' simply means 'fishing in the dark,'
which makes the work extremely hazardous.

MERCER 184

106 They Locked Me Up in Bonavist' Jail

Moses Harris
Lethbridge, 1977

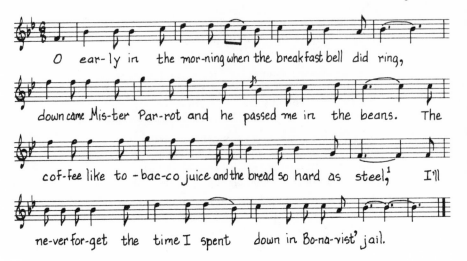

O ear-ly in the mor-ning when the breakfast bell did ring,
down came Mis-ter Par-rot and he passed me in the beans. The
cof-fee like to-bac-co juice and the bread so hard as steel,[1] I'll
ne-ver for-get the time I spent down in Bo-na-vist' jail.

2 O they locked me up in Bonavist' Jail, the key upon the wall,
A hundred and fifty bedbugs playing a game of ball;
The coffee like tobacco juice and the bread so hard as steel,
They locked me up in Bonavist' Jail and threw away the keys.

1 'Steel' is pronounced 'stayle' to rhyme with jail.

I don't know whether other verses exist to this song and these were the only ones Uncle
Mose could remember, or if these verses are the only ones. Uncle Mose knew a store of
these ditties, some of which were used to accompany tunes. Apart from being a good
singer, he could also play a variety of musical instruments – fiddle, accordion, mouth-
organ, handsaw, and others he himself invented from cans, bottles, etc. The first violin he
ever played he made himself: he was at a dance one night where a man was playing a
fiddle; he asked to borrow it for a few minutes during the break, ran home, and traced its
shape out on some cardboard. He made the fiddle soon after and taught himself to play.

182

107 Thomas and Nancy

Annie Green
Francois, 1977

Undulating

In Bris-tol there lived a fair dam-sel; and
she being a beau-ty most bright, a
sai- lor he loved her fond com- pany far
dearer than he loved his own life.

2 But when her old father he heard it
   Those words unto her he did say;
   'I'll send you far from your own country
   And I'll send that young sailor to sea.'

3 He pressed this fair maid to his bosom
   And the tears down her cheeks fast did fall;
   He kissed her cold lips and they parted
   And he bid her a loving farewell.

4 'O Thomas, o Thomas,' cried Nancy,
   'We have vowed that we never would part';
   She fell on the beach broken-hearted
   And the tears from her blue eyes did start.

5 Our ship reached the port and returning
   Like some sea-bird she danced o'er the foam;
   While Thomas lay on his soft pillow,
   Dreamt of Nancy and parents at home.

6 There was lightning and loud peals of thunder,
   There was lightning flashed over the main;
   Where the rocks split our good ship asunder,
   And the crew found a watery grave.

7 To the beach, to the beach Nancy often had visited
   She beheld a most pitiful sight,
   'Twas the corpse of her Thomas they carried
   To the place where they oft-times had been.

8 Next day there were two loyal lovyers
Cut down in the height of their bloom;
It's been said that they loved one another
And was both buried into one tomb.

This was the first song I heard Annie Green sing, and she sang it beautifully while providing a rhythmical accompaniment with the motion of her rocking-chair. This gave the impression of the sound of a ship upon the sea; her timbers creaking as she rolled gently in the waves.

MERCER 185

108 The *Thomas J. Hodder*

Johnny Tobias Pearson and others
Southeast Bight, 1977

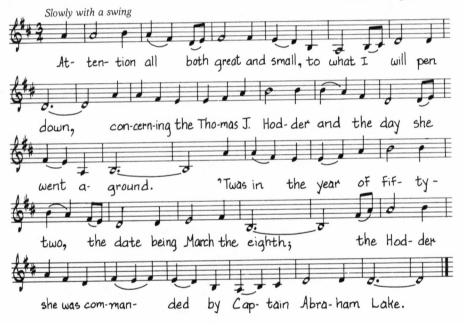

Slowly with a swing

At-ten-tion all both great and small, to what I will pen down, con-cern-ing the Tho-mas J. Hod-der and the day she went a-ground. 'Twas in the year of fif-ty-two, the date being March the eighth; the Hod-der she was com-man-ded by Cap-tain Abra-ham Lake.

2 The *Hodder* she is a splendid boat, about one hundred ton,
A. Wareham he is her owner and she's always on the run
From Spencer's Cove to Boston and manys another port,
For use in exportation and also for import.

3 She left the port of Sydney with a full cargo on board;
'Twas coal, provisions and groceries combined made up her load.
The next day leaving Burin her crew was gay and bright
Not thinking any accident would happen in broad daylight.

4 She steamed along and all went well 'til Paradise grew near.
Said Abe unto his boys: 'I think we'll go the course in here.
I've been here manys the time before, it is a real short cut.'
The *Hodder* was deeply loaded and she grounded in Lake's Gut.

5 The news was soon flashed o'er the air by means of ship-to-shore,
A. Wareham was soon contacted, saying: 'The *Hodder* is doomed I'm sure;
She's high and dry here in Lake's Gut, her bottom is gone, I know,
So come and bring assistance if you want to save her load.'

6 From Paradise and vicinity the people then did come,
To help their well-known captain and see what could be done.
But when they drew 'longside of her on him they saw no frown:
'Load up your punts and dories, b'ys, the *Hodder* is going down.'

7 Provisions were quickly taken from out of her afterhold;
There's punts and dories loaded, and some of them took coal.
There's men from Toslow and Bona, Paradise and Petit Forte –
Doctor Wilson he was also there to help in his little boat.

8 A. Wareham was soon expected for to come around the bill
The tide it was also rising, which favoured the *Hodder* well.
At six o'clock she floated, and under her own spark;
Steamed down to Little Paradise and tied up to the wharf.

9 He stayed there for a short while to see if she would leak,
But Abe was discontented [and] for the Burin dock did leave.
He said: 'My b'ys let go her lines; before dark we will make.'
But to his great misfortune he runned her on the Pancake.

10 A. Wareham was crossing the harbour in the *Evette* when she struck.
I'm sure he must be thinking by now that the *Hodder* is having tough luck;
But when he stepped in on her deck he showed no sign of grief,
For manys the boat of Wareham's was lost upon some reef.

11 The wind being from the Nor'west as smooth as oil could be,
And all the men around there, their minds from work were free;
They all agreed to lend a hand to take her off the 'Cake,
To assist Alberto Wareham and also Captain Lake.

12 Well after a long while tugging 'twas off the rock did slide.
He then proceeded to Spencer's Cove with the *Evette* close 'longside.
A. Wareham contacted his firm for to have a crew at hand,
To finish discharging her cargo as soon as she did land.

13 The *Hodder* is now on Burin dock for repairs we understand,
And soon she will resume her voyage with Abe still in command.
We wish him luck with all our hearts for he is liked by all;
Misfortunes they can happen to the greatest and the small.

This song was composed by Lil Fitzgerald and Rose Pickett, formerly the Brennan sisters of Paradise, Placentia Bay. Mr Power learned this song from the late Anthony Ward of Southeast Bight. The *Hodder* is the most requested song at any party in the area.

109 The Tobacco Song

Anita Best
St John's, 1977

Ye fel-lows smokes to-bac-co, come pi-ty my case, I'm
here on this is-land with-out a damn taste; sur-
-roun-ded be ice and en-com-passed with snow, in
search of that weed I don't know where to go.

2 O the great God of Heaven have pity on I,
   And send me some 'baccy or else I will die;
   'Tis six weeks or better since I had a draw,
   And I can't remember when I had a chaw.

3 Ye fellows smokes tea, well ye'd better beware
   It is very scarce and most damnable dear,
   And to my opinion a good cup of tea
   Would suit you far better than to smoke it away.

4 Ye fellows smokes moss, the worse robbers of all
   Goes away with their bags picking that in the Fall;
   If they'd leave it alone, sure 'twould keep their house tight,
   But they're only just making a fool of the pipe.

5 I can't smoke the stuff I sees some people smoke
   Such as withrod and shavings and strands of old rope;
   Some they do say wax it is good to chaw,
   But it loosens your teeth – puts a kink in your jaw.

6 If the wind veers northeast then the ice it will go,
   We'll all get some 'baccy St Peter's I know;
   Every man with his tavern stuck out of his gob,
   And to hell we'll shove shavings, spruce rind and withrod!

This is a popular song in Placentia Bay which is often bewildering to those not familiar
with certain terms: 'withrod' is a common enough plant in Newfoundland, some call it the
wild raisin – it has the unfortunate fragrance of cat's piss; 'shavings' are pieces of kindling
wood which have been 'shaved' out on the end so that curls of wood are still attached; a
'draw' is a smoke from either a pipe or a cigarette and a 'chaw' is a chew of tobacco;

'spruce rind' is the bark of the spruce tree; 'moss' was used to fill up the spaces between the 'studs' of old houses. The 'studs' were round sticks flattened on two sides and nailed together vertically to form the wall of the house; 'tavern' is a 'type of clay pipe they used to get in St Pierre' (a French island off the south coast of Newfoundland, often called St Peter's by Newfoundlanders).

Peter Leonard wrote this song after ice had drifted into Placentia Bay and blocked up most of the harbours on Isle Valen, where he lived.

The air is not the original one I learned from Pius Power, but one of my own. A.B.

110 Tobias Murphy and Tom Hann

Pius Power, Sr
Southeast Bight, 1983

Moderate; free swing

'Twas in the month of Sep-tem-ber, the date I can-not give, when e-very-thing up-on the sea have found it hard to live, where boats and schoo-ners found it bad, and al-so bri-gan-tines, a-round the shores of New-found-land the like was sel-dom seen.

2 There's two captains in particular, their names I will send forth –
Tobias Murphy from The Rams, Tom Hann from Petit Forte.

3 As they were out on St Mary's banks when the gale began to rise,
They quickly got under way for to save their precious lives;
In under a double-reef foresail they runned before wind and sea,
And the first landfall I believe Tom saw was the point of Golden Bay.

187

4 For they were in quite handy and the morning it was thick,
  With wind and tide upon both sides, it hove a heavy kick;
  They hoisted a three-reef mainsail to clear in around the Cape,
  It was their only chance, my b'ys, from danger to escape.

5 But when he got her in around it was to his greatest shock,
  When a heavy sea broke on the boat, Tom thinks 'twas Brierly Rock.

6 For about three quarters of an hour and the sea in mountains foamed,
  When those poor b'ys gave up their lives and all their friends at home.
  The people on the shore that day they turned their backs around,
  Not to behold that dreadful sight of their own friends sinking down.

7 The priest he read the rosary, it was read in open air,
  The Holy Mother raised her hand and brought her children clear.

8 Tobias Murphy he made low and also was too late
  For the wind it caught him on the veer before he reached the Cape;
  In under a two-reef foresail he was forced to bear away,
  And run her for North Harbour down in St Mary's Bay.

9 Now Peter Murphy he took charge, we thought him best to steer.
  Our compass and binnacle it was gone and the morning wasn't clear.
  But that poor fellow hadn't long charge when dismal was his doom –
  A heavy sea broke over her and swept him to his doom.

10 I'm sure the like had never runned in his strong heart or mind,
   For he done his whole endeavour when he saw that sea behind;
   Din Bruce he runned to help him not thinking that he'd go,
   But a broken sea swept them away some fathoms down below.

11 It was terrible on board the boat that day for to see those two men drown,
   Our boat was overpowered in sea and she would not come around;
   Our boat got overpowered in sea and so seldom would she breathe,
   As we left those poor fellows far behind in a wide and a watery grave.

12 And such another gale as that on the coast was seldom seen –
   May the Lord have mercy on the souls of those two fishermen.

According to Aunt Carrie Brennan, this sea tragedy occurred in 1878: 'The priest was having Mass in Lear's Cove near Cape St Mary's – that was the Cape they were rounding – when the storm arose. Some men went in and said: "Father, there's a boat in dire distress out in the bay." The priest got ready and went out, and the wind blowing a gale – he got down on his knees and prayed to the blessèd Virgin and our blessèd Mother raised Her hand and brought Her children free.' Aunt Carrie has the following lines as the beginning of the first verse:

Come all ye hearty fishermen and listen unto me
While I relate the dangers that do attend the sea

The song was composed by Peter Leonard whom Mr Power learned it from. 'The last time I heard him sing "Tobias Murphy" 'twas in the '30s – I was in my twenties. That was the night we had the soup supper in Clattice Harbour that he made the song about. He sung it [the Soup Supper in Clattice Harbour] for us on the way home from Mass in St Kyran's the next Sunday.' Peter Leonard was called Gandy.

Singer's key D♭

111 Trois Navires de Blé

Guillaume (Willie) Robin
Port au Port Peninsula, 1972

Assez vif

Un gros coup de vent de nor-det trois na-vires de blé s'en fit ren-trer[1]

Trois na-vires de blé s'en fit ren-trer, nous i-rons jou-er

sur le bord de l'eau, nous i-rons jou-er dans l' î- le.

2 Trois filles d'un roi veulent marchander
Nous irons jouer sur le bord de l'eau   >*bis*
Nous irons jouer sur le bord de l'eau
Nous irons jouer dans l'île.

3 La plus jeune avait l'pied léger
A bord d'la barque elle a sauté
A bord d'la barque elle a sauté
Nous irons jouer dans l'île.

4 Combien le vendez-vous votre blé
Nous irons jouer sur le bord de l'eau
Oh-oh six sous le boisseau
Nous irons jouer dans l'île.

5 N'est pas trop cher s'il est bon blé
Nous irons jouer sur le bord de l'eau
N'est pas trop cher s'il est bon blé
Nous irons jouer dans l'île.

6 Marin, marin cessez d'voguer
Nous irons jouer sur le bord de l'eau
J'entends ma mère m'app'ler pour souper
Nous irons jouer dans l'île.

7 J'entends ma mère m'app'ler pour souper
Nous irons jouer sur le bord de l'eau
Et ainsi les petits enfants pleurer
Nous irons jouer dans l'île.

8 Oh-oh la belle vous mentissez[2]
Jamais d'enfants vous n'avez eu
Mais preste à Dieu[3] vous n'en aurez
Nous irons jouer sur le bord de l'eau
Nous irons jouer dans l'île.

9 Ils porteront chapeau brodé
   Nous irons jouer sur le bord de l'eau
   Et boucles d'argent à leurs souliers
   Nous irons jouer dans l'île.

1 S'en furent rentrer
2 Mentez
3 Plut à Dieu

The number of lines in each verse varies throughout the song; the air has been transcribed so as to accommodate the first verse. Anyone wishing to sing the song may want to regularize it somewhat to suit their own singing style.

   The song was collected by Gerald Thomas.

112 The Wreck of the *Union* (A)

Moses Harris
Lethbridge, 1976

Ye lands-men and ye lands-men bold, it's lit-tle do youse know what us poor sai-lors do en-dure when the stor-my winds do blow.

2 You can stay on shore with your pretty girls
   Tell unto them fond tales,
   But the hardest labour that ever you done
   Was to reap your own corn fields.

3 The eighteenth day of November past
   A heavy gale came on,
   The heavens above looked angry
   And the clouds did shade the sun.

4 Our captain gived us orders
   And orders we must obey;
   'You'd better go forward, my boys,' he said,
   'Your foresail to lower away.'

5 We tried to reef our mainsail
  We found it couldn't be done;
  'Twas under a three-reef foresail, my boys
  Six leagues to the sea she runned.

6 Three hours in that condition
  She had no means to stay,
  To see the seas come tumbling down
  Our ship on her beam-ends lay.

7 Once more she gently rises
  Which caused us all to say:
  'God bless our noble vessel, my boys,
  Once more she heads the sea.'

8 We boarded the wreck in the morning
  A dismal sight to behold;
  Three men lay frozen at her pumps
  Six more in the cabin lay cold.

9 She is the *Union* from St John's
  How well I knows her mould,
  And every time I thinks on her distress
  She makes my blood run cold.

10 She is the *Union* from St John's
  How well I knows her name,
  And every night as I lay on my bed
  I can hear the young widows complain.

11 So now they're gone God bless them –
  My boys your race is run;
  A widow must weep for her husband dear
  And mourn for her darling son.

The Wreck of the *Union* (B)

Pius Power, Sr
Southeast Bight, 1980

1 Ye fishermen of Newfoundland
  Come listen to what I write,
  'Twas in ploughing over the salt, salt sea
  In that I took delight.

2 I was once as hearty a sailor lad
  As ever unfurled a sail,
  But the hardest labour I ever done
  Was to reef an unfurling sail.

3 'Twas on the fourteenth of January past
   When the gale it did come on,
   The elements looked angry (on us)
   And the clouds o'er cast the sun.

4 You may be on shore with your pretty girls
   Telling to them fond tales,
   But the hardest labour that ever you done
   Was to reap your own corn fields.

5 With the wind about east and be soud' me b'ys
   And also heavy showers of hail,
   The night it got dark and stormy
   And 'twas on a leeshore we did tail.

6 Our captain give us orders
   And that we should obey,
   Our captain he give orders
   Our foresail to cut away.

7 We tried to take our foresail in
   'Twas more than we could do,
   We hoisted our jib right manfully
   And rounded our good ship to.

8 See how she slowly rises
   Which caused all hands to say:
   'God bless our noble vessel, me b'ys
   Once more she heads the sea.'

9 We tried to take that foresail in
   It really couldn't be done!
   We hoisted our three-reef mainsail
   Five leagues o'er the sea she runned.

10 'Twas early next morning
   We received our greatest shock –
   We saw a craft on her beam-ends
   Three leagues from Mount Bernard Rock.

11 We boarded her immejitely
   To get what (re)marks we could
   There's three lashed frozen to each pump
   Five more in her cabin was dead.

12 See how the tiller works over them
   And that most wondrous rare,
   And the gooseneck marked on the head of it
   Where those fishermen used to steer.

13 She is the *Union* from St John's
   'Tis well I knows her name,
   And every night when I lie on my bed
   I can hear their young widows complain.

14 She is the *Union* from St John's
Right well I knows her mould,
And when I thinks on those poor b'ys
It makes my blood run cold.

15 She's gone, she's gone, forever she's gone!
I know their glass was run,
The widow must weep for her husband
And the mother her darling son.

An American broadside ballad 'The Wreck of the Brig *Union*' was discovered by Fannie
Hardy Eckstorm and Mary Winslow Smyth and printed in their book *Minstrelsy of Maine* in
1927. According to them, the song was written in the early 1800s. However, the ship could
possibly have been from Newfoundland since there were two (and possibly more) wrecks
recorded of ships named the *Union* from Newfoundland around that time.

Mr Power's version is the closest of the two to the original broadside, which has Mount
Desert's Rock instead of Mount Bernard Rock. He learned the song from his Uncle Dave
Brewer when he was but a child of nine or ten. 'When Uncle Dave got a drop in, this was
the song he would always sing . . . it was the only one he had.'

We did not include both airs since they are almost identical.

MERCER 190

113 The Valley of Kilbride

Dorman Ralph
St John's, 1976

On the bat- tle field in sun-ny France a he- ro brave did
stand; he thought of friends he loved so well in
dear old New-found- land, when a vi- sion bright did
gain his view, the dear old ri- ver- side, and the
home he loved in boy-hood days in the val- ley of Kil- bride.

2 A comrade he lay wounded, lay dying on the field.
Those plucky Newfoundlanders, they died before they yielded;
On no-man's land they rushed across, where shot and shell do fly,
On no-man's land they rushed across, you could hear their charging cry.

3 No coward's blood runs through their veins, they'll conquer now or die.
They gained the front line trenches from the enemy that day;
While on their right and on their left, machine guns they did fly,
When a dying comrade raised his head, a signal to draw nigh.

4 He says, 'Dear Jack, those parting words I want for you to hear.'
He says, 'Dear Jack, those parting words I want for you to know.'
He says, 'Dear Jack, those parting words I want for you to tell
To my father and my mother, likewise my sister Nell.

5 Tell mother not to weep for me but pray for me each day,
And whisper words of comfort, Jack, to her that's far away;
And whisper words of comfort, Jack, and take her by the hand,
And tell her in that July Drive, how bravely I did stand.

6 There's another one who waits for me, and thinks that I'll come home;
Go and tell her that in Bowring Park we never more shall roam.
We never more shall meet on earth, since you and I must part,
But still her memory lingers yet, within my bleeding heart.

7 There's a photo that she gave to me lies closely by my side,
You can scarcely recognize it now for with my blood it's dyed;
You can scarcely recognize it now, but you will [be] sure to know,
It's a photo that she gave to me not a few short months ago.'

8 His voice grew weak, he scarce could speak, he freely grasped my hand,
He says, 'Dear Jack do not forget to bring tidings to Newfoundland,'
He says, 'Dear Jack do not forget how the blood flowed from my side;
God comfort my dear mother in the Valley of Kilbride.

9 I know that you will miss me Jack for soon we have to part.
I know that I won't live long with the pain that's in my heart;
I know that I am dying with the pain that's in my side,
My home I never more will see in the Valley of Kilbride.

10 I know that you will miss me Jack when you are all alone.
My grave will be in sunny France far from my native home.
My grave will be in sunny France way out on no-man's land,
And the dark-haired girl will weep for me in dear old Newfoundland.'

This song was possibly written by Johnny Burke. Uncle Mose Harris calls the 'plucky Newfoundlanders' (verse 2, line 2) 'plucky Terra Noviers (Novians)' and adds this extra verse:

Out of that drive five came alive I'm sorry for to say.
O'Donnell he was our captain, he stepped into the fray,
And to those few survivors leaved he did extend his hand
And he said: 'Brave boys I'm proud of youse and dear ol' Newfoundland.'

MERCER 342

114 Le Vingt-cinq de Juillet

Guillaume (Willie) Robin
Port au Port Peninsula, 1971

Le vingt-cinq de juil-let-(te) du Cap nos sons[1] par-tis, le vingt-cinq de juil-le-(te) du Cap nos sons par-tis, du Cap nos sons par-tis et a-vec gran-de jouis-san-ce. C'é-tait pour al-ler voir[2] nos jo-lies mâî-tresses en Fran-ce.

2 En arrivant-z-en large-z-en large en pleine mer
   Nous 'ons 'trapé[3] une bordée de vent à la Bouline
   Que le petit navire avait les bords à la mer(e).

3 Les matelots dans les hunes craient-z-à haute voix (bis)
   Que Dieu nous fasse la grâce de tiendre[4] un bout de câble. (bis)

4 La tempête est pássée et garçons faut s'remonter
   Il faut virer les voiles[5] et ainsi appareiller(e)
   Ainsi appareiller pour la jolie Rochelle.

5 En arrivant-z-au havre a tiré trois coups d'canon
   Tiré trois coups d'canon et c'est pour faire à savoir[6]
   Qu'un navire arrive-z-arrive et à bon port(e).

6 Arrivé-z-à bon port(e) chargé d'une[7] marchandise
   Chargé d'une marchandise et une quantité d'argent(e)
   Les filles de la Rochelle avec[8] leurs hommes montaient à bord;
   Il faut donc aller dire à Monsieur la Galichesse
   Que son navire arrive-z-arrive et-z-à bon port(e).

7 Preste à Dieu[9] ça c'est vrai et que mon navire arrive
   Que mon navire arrive et arrive et-z-à bon port(e)
   Chargé d'une marchandise et une quantité d'argent.

1 Nous sommes   4 Pronounced tchinde   7 Pronounced eune
2 Pronounced ouère   5 Pronounced vouèles   8 Pronounced ac
3 Nous avons attrapé   6 Pronounced savouère   9 Plut à Dieu

Final 'e' is usually pronounced or added where it is not normally present to fit the melody of the song. 'Z' is a liaison sound used by the singer. The addition of these syllables does not affect the pronunciation of preceding letters, which would usually be silent. Port(e) = por-e.

The number of lines in each verse of the song is irregular and does not always conform to the number of lines in the tune. This practice, however, seems to be consistent with the singer's style.

The song was collected by Gerald Thomas.

115 The Virgin on the Strand

Pius Power, Sr
Southeast Bight, 1978

The star of eve rose glo-rious-ly, o-ver-spread the bri-ny waves, when on a green and mos-sy bank the vir-gin kneeled to pray; it was oft-times called the Mos-sy Green, that Vir-gin Ma-ry's spot, and the bank of green where Ma-ry kneeled was the bright-est of them all.

2 When slowly over the ocean, a goodlye barque appeared;
  Her joyful crew stood on the deck as to the land she steered.
  Her milk-white sails overspread the deep, shined in the briny sea –
  Her keel was steady in the deep and motionless she lay.

3 Our captain saw the Lady as she kneeled there to pray.
  He marked the whiteness of her robes and the brightness of her brow;
  With her hands enfolded in fervent prayer upon her milk-white breast,
  And her meek eyes cast to heaven, where her soul lay at rest.

4 Our captain saw the Lady calling his joyful crew –
  When on that lonely Virgin they give loud mocking jeer;
  For such another female kind they never saw before,
  And they cursed the faint and lagging breeze that kept them from the shore.

5 O the Lady she had left the strand and vanished from their view –
   She spread her white wings o'er the deep, most gloriously to view;
   She spread her white wings over the deep and over the coral sand,
   But our captain died before he reached the Virgin on the strand.

6 The ocean from its bosom then shook out all moonlight shades –
   The thunder increased tremendously and furious ran the waves;
   The thunder increased tremendously and the lightning rent in shock,
   When our brave craft in pieces went on Inchechainey [sic] Rock.

7 It was early next morning 'twas dismal for to view,
   And buried there all in the sand was the captain and his crew;
   Which is often called the Mossy Green where the Virgin she did stand –
   But our captain died before he reached the Virgin on the strand.

Under the title 'The Virgin Mary's Bank,' this song appeared in *Irish Com-All-Ye's* (1901) by
Manus O'Conor. In the table of contents, O'Conor lists the author of the song as
J.J. Callanan. Inchidony's Rock is the place-name given in the Irish version. Mr Power
learned the song from Mr Bill Flynn of Petit Forte.

116 The *Water Witch*

Pius Power, Sr
Southeast Bight, 1980

Irregular – slow

Come all ye true-born fish-er-men and lis-ten to my song, I
hope ye'll pay at- ten- tion, I won't de- lay you long. You
all re- mem- ber Pouch Cove and those true-born sons so brave, who
saved the crew of the Wa- ter Witch, so near a wa- tery grave.

2 On Christmas Eve that craft did leave when loud the wind did roar.
   'Twas on a reef she came to grief not far from Pouch Cove shore,
   A place they call the Horrid Gulch the schooner headed on,
   And in the twinkling of an eye three poor, dear souls were gone.

197

3 Three seamen from the *Water Witch* leaped when they heard the shock;
The rest belong to that doomed ship were hurled on the rock,
To wait three hours in storms and showers, and loud the sea did dash;
They see their schooner breaking up, hard on the rocks did smash.

4 The Pouch Cove fishermen to a man turned out that cruel night.
For those who gazed on those poor souls, it was a doleful sight;
And for to make the scene much worse poor females numb with cold
Was waiting there to be relieved by those brave heroes bold.

5 Punts, rhodes and lanterns they were brought by kind and willing hands,
The shrieks of females in distress those fishermen could not stand.
And for to face that Horrid Gulch six hundred feet did go
To save those souls half-dead with cold who waited down below.

6 Brave Alfred Moore, a Pouch Cove man: 'I'll take the lead,' he cried,
When around his waist strong hempen rope in double knots was tied;
And now strong men are on the top to lower him over the cliff
To dash our hero down below, in blinding snow and drift.

7 Three times they swung him in the dark in blinding drift and snow,
Before his foot could get a place to give him any hold;
At length he found one resting place close to a sheltered stone
Where he could see those souls below and hear their dismal moans.

8 Oh now to save this shipwrecked crew their hearts were filled with hope;
Six more brave Pouch Cove fishermen like heroes manned the rope.
And now some small handlines, like Moore, they managed for to lower
'Til all the *Water Witch*'s crew were landed safe on shore.

9 O hark! another scream was heard – the people got a shock –
Another female left below to perish on the rock!
When Alfred made another dash, and loud the wind did roar,
And took the woman in his arms in safety to shore.

10 The news was soon in Town next day about the *Water Witch*
The whole community got a shock, the poor as well as rich;
The Governor he sent home these words in letters bold and grand
To tell the pluck of these fishermen belong to Newfoundland.

11 The Humane Society of Liverpool, they very soon sent here
Gold medals to those fishermen who never knew no fear;
The Governor's lady pinned them on, those medals rare and rich,
To the Pouch Cove men who saved the lives aboard the *Water Witch*.

12 Oh here's success to those brave boys who risked in storm and breeze
Their precious lives to save those souls who ventured over the sea.
May peace and plenty be their lot, that gay and gallant band –
Brave Alfred Moore and all the rest belong to Newfoundland.

Mr Power learned 'The *Water Witch*' from his Uncle Frank: he presumed the ship left England for Newfoundland but went aground in Pouch Cove, that the loss occurred in 1875, and that she belonged to Cupids. However, in *When Was That?* Mosdell says the *Water Witch*, a Brigus schooner commanded by Captain Spracklin, was lost at Pouch Cove with nine persons on 29 November 1873; eleven lives were saved by Alfred Moore.

MERCER 151

117 The Waterford Strike

Anthony Ward
St John's, 1979

1 'Twas over at the Waterford now just one month ago,
For pension rights to fit their jobs the staff on strike did go,
And out to man the picket lines went guys and gals alike,
All knew they'd soon be needed – it would be a short-lived strike.

2 But then up through their picket lines the 'Meter Maids' all came,
Union Members every one – they crossed through just the same
To do the jobs of those on strike and leave them without power,
With nothing left to bargain with – this is NAPE's darkest hour.

3 With Management and Cops inside, the strikers on the line,
Bill Doody says he'll never budge, no changes will he sign –
He swears the Waterford compares with the General or the Grace,
But he needs cops to do their jobs to take the strikers place.

4 It's Civil Service Hockey time – the cops and boys in red,
Are playing in the Finals with the 'Fuzz' one game ahead;
The fans include a number from the Waterford to cheer,
And hope the 'Fire Boys' can beat Bill Doddy's scabs this year.

5 And win they do, a shut one, they put six in past the cops,
Who take the loss with such poor grace that gloves and sticks are dropped;
The fans are treated to the sight of sportsmanship outlawed –
Those big, brave cops won't leave the rink without their Riot Squad!!!

6 Yes, three cars and the paddy wagon jammed with riot gear,
Forty to arrest one Union man who is in the clear.
Dozens in their helmets to escort their beaten chums;
Respect for them died on the spot – they proved they're 'Doody's Chums.'

7 So now each day at eight and four, and midnight for new shifts,
The riot boys are there in force all swinging billy sticks.
Then paydays those 'scab dollars' flow with cops all 'round the place,
They've even shaken paycheques in a Union Member's face!

8 'Tis sad to see it come to this, the bitterness will last
Long after Doody gets some sense, and striking days are past.
The Union guys and gals who lost, their families did without,
Will long remember Hawco's boys inside while they were OUT.

9 The Union feels they have the right to fight for what is just –
We live in a democracy where freedom is a must;
If they aren't doing jobs the equal of the 'boys in blue,'
Why aren't the nurses left to handle patients 'til it's through?

10 So now the cops keep order, and they're taking home the pay
Of fellow Union Members, but I hope to see the day
When Hawco and his 'Doody boys' are striking then we'll see
The guys they crossed at Waterford will all be cops – FOR FREE!!!

This song was composed by Anthony Ward and a group of friends about a strike by the employees of the Waterford Hospital, St John's, in 1977. The strike lasted four months.

118 Wave over Wave

Jim Payne (CAPAC)
St John's, 1983

Me name's A-bel Ro-gers, a share-man am I on a three-mas-ted schoo-ner from Twi-lin-gate Isle; I've been the world o-ver north, south, east, and west but the mid-dle of no-where's where I like it best. *Refrain:* Where it's wave o-ver wave, sea o-ver bow I'm as hap-py a man as the sea will al-low; there's no o-ther life for a sai-lor like me but to sail the salt sea, boys, sail the sea, there's no o-ther life but to sail the salt sea.

2 The work it is hard and the hours are long
My spirit is willing, my back it is strong;
And when our work's over then whiskey we'll pour
We'll dance with the girls upon some foreign shore.

Chorus: Where it's wave over wave, sea over bow
I'm as happy a man as the sea will allow;
There's no other life for a sailor like me
But to sail the salt sea, boys, sail the sea –
There's no other life but to sail the salt sea.

3 I'd leave my wife lonely ten months of the year
She made me a home and raised my children dear,
But she'd never come out to bid farewell to me
Or ken why a sailor must sail the salt sea.

4 I've sailed the wide ocean four decades or more
And many times wondered what I do it for;
I don't know the answer it's pleasure and pain
With life to live over I'd do it again.

This is a contemporary folk-style song composed by Jim Payne, formerly of Pilly's Island in
Notre Dame Bay. Jim often performs it in the local pubs and bars together with local
musician Kelly Russell.

119 We Left the Port of Sydney

Mary Ann Skinner
Francois, 1977

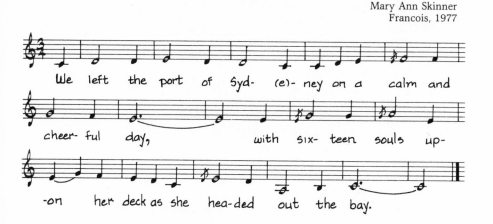

We left the port of Syd- (e)- ney on a calm and
cheer- ful day, with six- teen souls up-
-on her deck as she hea-ded out the bay.

2 We had a load of coal on board
Bound for Argentia fair,
The extra men on board of her
Bound for homes and loved ones dear.

3 We had not long been sailing
When a thunder-storm arose,
The lightening flashed about her deck
As if fighting with the foes.

4 The skipper he came up on deck
And the other men likewise,
And with his wise old mind, he said:
'A storm is brewing boys.'

5 I think we better go below
And put our oilskins on,
And then tie up our mainsail
Before the storm comes on.

6 'Twas down below those men did go
Without a thought of fear,
The danger that awaited them
Upon the ocean there.

7 When suddenly a mighty crash
That filled the heavy air,
And sank the ship with mighty force
And threw her in despair.

8 The seas closed in upon her
And she sank beneath the waves,
The men below her deck were trapped
And no time their lives to save.

9 The extra men on board of her
As passengers did go,
And they to save their money
For their families that we know.

10 They left their homes in early March
And to Lunenburg did go,
To drag their living from the banks
Or from the watery foe.

11 The fishery being a poor one
As many can relate,
And they to save their money
Meet this terrible sad fate.

12 And now to those who mourn for them
They never more shall see,
God grant them rest and comfort
And the tenderest sympathy.

13 On earth we'll part and separate
In heaven we'll meet again,
Where there will be no sorrow
And no thought of coming pain.

14 The ocean then her dead shall heal
And we shall all unite,
And dwell within the city
In that land of pure delight.

Because there is no mention of the name of the ship or the captain in this song, it is difficult to trace any information about it. This is rather unusual for locally composed songs concerning sea disasters which normally name either the ship involved, the captain of the vessel, or even some of the crew members themselves.

120 Why Don't Father's Ship Come In?

Annie Green
Francois, 1977

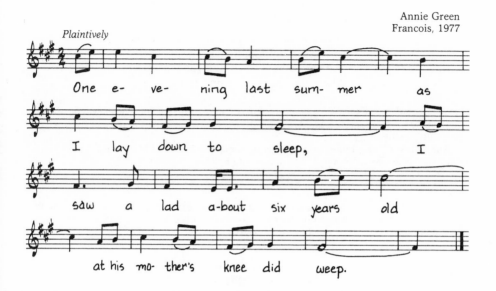

Plaintively

One e- ve- ning last sum- mer as

I lay down to sleep, I

saw a lad a-bout six years old

at his mo- ther's knee did weep.

2 'O why don't father's ship come in
   And why don't he come home,
   While other ships are sailing in
   Spreading the ocean foam.

3 'For he said, six months he would be gone
   Leaving you and I alone,
   And through the long dark winter nights
   Six months have passed and gone.

4 'So why don't father's ship come in
   O mother come tell me why,
   O why don't father's ship come in
   What makes you weep and cry?'

5 'My boy your father's long voyage is o'er
   You'll never see him no more,
   For he and his tall gallant ship
   Will never reach the shore. .

6 For the ship and all of her cargo
   Went down in the ocean deep,
   And the seas are rolling mountains high
   O'er the graves where they do sleep.'

7 'If this be so, dear mother,' he cried,
   'From the grave they cannot come,
   And you and I are left alone
   For to lament and mourn.

8 'How well can I remember
  When he nursed me on his knee,
  And brought to me some buds and flowers
  From off the Indian tree.'

9 'My boy you're the pride of all my heart,'
  As she pressed him to her breast,
  And closed her eyes to the yonder skies
  Where the weary ones find rest.

This was one of Annie Green's favourite songs. There is a large body of such songs which are sung with great emotion and are evidently very meaningful to the men and women who often call for them.

   Annie Green learned most of her songs from her father, Aunt Clare Carter, and her husband, who was a fine singer and accordion player.

Uncle Mose Harris said that, traditionally, at the end of each song, a singer would sing this verse to let the man or woman of the house know that his glass needed filling. Therefore, it appropriately marks the conclusion of our songbook.

It's a very good song, and it's very well sung
Very good company every one –
He that can mend it is welcome to try,
But always remember the singer is dry!

Glossary of unfamiliar words

Many of the definitions used here have been cited directly from the *Dictionary of Newfoundland English* (Toronto 1982), edited by G.M. Story, W.J. Kirwin, and J.D.A. Widdowson

bawn Expanse of rocks on which salted cod are spread for the quick-drying process of the Labrador and Bank fisheries

bill (of a headland) The point of any headland or cape

bring to To come to anchor, to close with the land

caplin scull The migration of the caplin from the deep sea to inshore waters to spawn along the beaches; the period, usually June and July, when caplin spawn along the shore; also, the shoals of cod-fish which appear in coastal waters in pursuit of migrating caplin

copy (ice) To jump from one piece of floating ice or ice pan to another

dawny Sickly (pale), the nightmare, in a dream state; possibly from the Irish *donaidhe* – miserable, in poor health

fitted out Equipped with gear, furnished with supplies or provisions – that is, a boat is fitted out for sea

flusterate Possibly resulting from a blend of fluster and frust(e)rate and having the combined meaning of both

glass is run The hour glass has run out; a metaphor for life is ended

grades of fish (salted cod): 1 Spanish 2 merchantable 3 Madeira 4 West Indies; fish was graded or culled depending on the market for which it was destined.

grum Said of a gloomy, morose person, or overcast or stormy weather

heave out To capsize or roll over

heave the lead to sound To throw out a line weighted with lead and marked in fathoms to judge depth of water

horse-pipe Corruption of hawse-pipe – a cast-iron pipe fitted into a hawse-hole (where the chain or cable goes out) to protect the wood

jack (boat) A bluff, two-masted decked vessel, schooner-rigged and varying from 5-20 tons; it carried one dory and three men, and usually had the rudder outside

jigger Unbaited weighted hook(s) used with a line to catch cod or squid by giving a sharp, upward jerk

jumbo The largest and most inboard jib on a sailing schooner: it is attached to a boom and swings in over the deck; the other jibs are attached outside it; it is often used with a riding sail

lace up a tow To fasten a number of seal pelts together at the edge, forming a 'tow' for hauling over the ice by a rope

(east) line An imaginary line extending in an easterly direction from the east point of the compass to the horizon

lines Single line with a hook attached and sometimes baited; a buoyed line of great length to which short lines (suds/seds) with baited hooks are attached at intervals

out in the door Expression used in the sense of being thrown out of a place

pitch (of wind) To blow up suddenly from a certain direction; to strike

planter A settler in Newfoundland as opposed to a migratory English fisherman; a fisherman and owner of fishing premises, boat or small vessel who, supplied by a merchant, engages a crew to work on the share system; migratory fisherman from Newfoundland who conducts summer fishery from a 'station,' 'room,' or harbour on the coast of Labrador

prosition Possibly resulting from a blend of position and profession and having the combined meaning of both

punt An undecked boat up to 25 feet in length, round-bottomed and keeled, driven by oars, sails, or engine and used variously in the inshore or coastal fishery; in parts of Newfoundland, this boat is flat-bottomed and unkeeled

rails Pieces of hardwood fixed to the edge of a sailing vessel outlining the shape of the vessel: the rails are horizontal, the beams supporting them are called stanchions; the length of the beam of a vessel is proportional to the length of the stanchions, a 13-foot beam means a 13-inch stanchion

rode (rhode, road) Strong, tightly woven rope used especially to secure an anchor or grapnel by which a small boat is moored in the harbour or on the inshore fishing grounds

scote To strain, toil, work hard; to scramble, struggle

shareman Member of a fishing crew who receives a stipulated proportion of the profits of the voyage rather than wages

shucks Lumberman's leather mitts; the bottom or foot of a long rubber boot with the leg cut off

slouse To splash about in or under water

take gear To haul up lines, nets, etc., and remove any fish found there

tan Mixture of cutch, American bark, salt water, salt, Stockholm or gas tar, and spruce or juniper rind used to preserve twine

three-leg Uncompleted mesh of a fish-net, having three corner knots and one loose strand of twine

trace ... jibs To put the rolled sail in ropes and hoist it up so far on the stay, clear of the sea

tub Wooden vessel used to hold coiled trawl-lines, bait, or marketable fish

twine Hemp, cotton, or nylon thread, varying in the number of its twisted strands, used in making fish-nets

West Indies The worst cull or grade of dried and salted cod-fish shipped to the West Indies

Bibliography

Allingham, William, ed. *The Ballad Book*. London: Macmillan and Company, Limited 1907

Aston, John, ed. *Real Sailor Songs*. London: Broadsheet King, 15 Mortimer Terrace 1973

Burke, John, and George Oliver. *The People's Songster: Buyer's Guide and Gems of Poetry and Prose*. St John's: Burke and Oliver 1900

Casey, G.J. 'Traditions and Neighbourhoods: The Folklore of a Newfoundland Fishing Outport,' unpublished MA thesis, Memorial University of Newfoundland, 1971

Clements, Rex. *Manavilins*. London: Heath Cranton, Limited 1928

Cox, Gordon S.A. *Folk Music in a Newfoundland Outport*. Ottawa: National Museum of Man Mercury Series, Canadian Centre for Folk Culture Studies, Paper no 32, 1980

Creighton, Helen. *Songs and Ballads from Nova Scotia*. New York: Dover Publications Inc. 1966

Doyle, Gerald S. *Old-Time Songs and Poetry of Newfoundland*. St John's: Gerald S. Doyle Limited 1927, 1940, 1955, and 1966

Eckstorm, Fanny, and Mary Smyth. *Minstrelsy of Maine*. Boston: Houghton, Mifflin and Company 1927

Fowke, Edith. *The Penguin Book of Canadian Folk Songs*. Middlesex, England: Penguin Books 1973

Greenleaf, Elizabeth Bristol, and Grace Yarrow Mansfield, eds. *Ballads and Sea Songs of Newfoundland*. Cambridge: Harvard University Press 1933; reprinted Hatboro, Pa.: Folklore Associates 1968

Kendall, Victor. *Ships on the South West Coast of Newfoundland from 1861-1889*. St John's: Memorial University of Newfoundland, Maritime History Group Archive, Winter 1973

Leach, MacEdward. *Folk Ballads and Songs of the Lower Labrador Coast*. Ottawa: National Museum of Canada 1965

The Livyere, vol. 2, no 1. St John's: Leeward Publishing Limited, August-October 1982

Marcus, Geoffrey Jules. *Battle of Quiberon Bay, 1759*. London: Hollis and Carter 1960

Martin, Edwina. *1980 Calendar. Historic Newfoundland. The Coastal Boats*. Corner Brook: M & M Enterprises Limited 1979

Mercer, Paul. *Newfoundland Songs and Ballads in Print, 1842-1974; a title and first-line index*. St John's: Memorial University of Newfoundland Folklore and Language Publications, Bibliographical and Special Series no 6, 1979

Mosdell, H.M. *When Was That?* St John's: The Trade Printers and Publishers, Limited 1923

Motherwell, William. *Minstrelsy: Ancient and Modern*. Glasgow: John Wylie 1827

Murphy, James. *Songs and Ballads of Newfoundland, Ancient and Modern*. St John's: James Murphy 1902

Murphy, James. *Songs Their Fathers Sung. For Fishermen. Old Time Ditties*. St John's: James Murphy 1923

Ó Brádaigh, Seán, ed. *Songs of 1798: The Year of the French*. Dublin: Dúchas 1982

O'Conor, Manus. *Irish Com-All-Ye's and Ballads of Ireland*. New York: The Popular Publishing Company 1901

'Out of the Past – The Great Tragedy,' St John's *Daily News*, 28 March 1957

Paddock, Dr Harold. *A Dialect Survey of Carbonear, Newfoundland*. University of Alabama Press, a publication of the American Dialect Society, no 68, 1981

Parker, John P. *Sails of the Maritimes*. Scarborough, Ont.: McGraw-Hill Ryerson Limited 1976

Peacock, Kenneth. *Songs of the Newfoundland Outports*. 3 vols. Ottawa: National Museum of Canada 1965

Singleton, Lucille. *Wrecks and Charts 1831-1942*. St John's: Memorial University of Newfoundland, Maritime History Group Archive, December 1973

Story, G.M., W.J. Kirwin, and J.D.A. Widdowson, eds. *Dictionary of Newfoundland English*. Toronto: University of Toronto Press 1982

White, John. *John White's Collection of Johnny Burke Songs*. St John's: Harry Cuff Publications Limited 1982

White, R. *List of Wrecks on the Coast of Newfoundland to 31st December, 1903*. St John's: Centre for Newfoundland Studies, Queen Elizabeth II Library, Memorial University of Newfoundland, 1904

Williams, Ralph Vaughan, and A.L. Lloyd, eds. *The Penguin Book of English Folksongs*. Middlesex, England: Penguin Books 1959

Index of first lines

On the battle field in sunny France a hero brave did stand   193
On the deck of a recruiting ship a young man he did stand   161
On the eighteenth of November, as you all might remember   172
On the twenty-fifth of August the gale began to rise   9
Said the lord to his lady: 'I am going away ...'   61
Sit down, boys, and I'll sing youse a ditty   127
Sit down, boys, I'll sing you a ditty   129
The eighteenth day of December last in Torbay we did lay   18
The eleventh of June, boys, our anchors we weighed   64
There's a quiet little village in Bonavist' Bay   139
The star of eve rose gloriously, overspread the briny waves   196
'Tis of a comely maiden living by a riverside   42
'Twas in the month of September, the date I cannot give   187
'Twas in the town of Wexford they sentenced him to die   30
'Twas on October the twenty-second as you may understand   73
'Twas over at the Waterford now just one month ago   199
Un gros coup de vent de nordet trois navires de blé s'en fit rentrer   189
We left the port of Sydney on a calm and a cheerful day   201
We shipped with young Goodridge in the spring of the year   95
When I was young and innocent I left my happy home   174
Ye daring sons of Newfoundland, come listen unto me   178
Ye daring sons of Newfoundland, please hearken unto me   10
Ye feeling hearted mothers, I hope ye will attend   112
Ye fellows smokes tobacco, come pity my case   186
Ye fishermen of Newfoundland, come listen to what I write   191
Ye fishermen who know so well the dangers of the deep   122
Ye lads and lasses of Newfoundland, come listen to my sad tale   158
Ye lads and ye lasses, I pray pay attention   93
Ye landsmen and ye landsmen bold, it's little do youse know   190
Ye muses nine, let you combine and listen to my song   176
Ye muses nine with me combine your aid I do invite   123
Ye noble-hearted Christians I hope that you'll attend   70
Ye noble Newfoundlanders that suffered in the gale   58
Ye people all both great and small, I hope you will attend   153
Ye people all both great and small, I'll have you to understand   4
Ye people all both great and small, please hearken unto me   125
You asked me to sing you a song; I'll do the best I can   51
You landsmen who all work on shore, how little do you know   126
You people all both great and small I hope you will attend   49